The Art of Flying

Also by Robert N. Buck

Weather Flying
Flying Know-How

The Art of Flying

Robert N. Buck

An Eleanor Friede Book
THOMASSON-GRANT
Charlottesville, Virginia

Published in 1992 by Thomasson-Grant
Copyright ©1984 by Robert N. Buck

Illustration credits: pages 21, 23, 27, 34,
119 by Priscilla Becroft; pages 53, 67, 77,
153, 171 by Pierre Barre.

Any inquiries should be directed to:
Thomasson-Grant, Inc., One Morton Drive
Charlottesville, Virginia 22901
(804) 977-1780

Printed in the United States

99 98 97 96 95 94 93 92 1 2 3 4 5

Library of Congress
Cataloging-in-Publication Data

Buck, Robert N., 1914-
    The art of flying / Robert N. Buck.
        p. cm.
    "An Eleanor Friede book."
    Originally published : New York : Macmillan :
London : Collier Macmillan, ©1984.
    Includes index.
    ISBN 1-56566-005-6
    1. Airplanes--Piloting. I. Title.
    [TL710.B75 1992]
    629.132'52--dc20   91-46647
                                        CIP

For Jean—

Thank You

MY GRATITUDE to Jim Gannett, superb airman and Boeing Test Pilot retired, close friend of many years, for reading technical portions of the manuscript and making valuable suggestions—and Jean for close scrutiny of the manuscript and courageous suggestions to her cantankerous husband on syntax and clarity—and pilot-son Robert O. Buck for patiently reading it all and helping me stay on course.

Contents

FEDERAL AVIATION REGULATIONS

91.3 Responsibility and Authority of Pilot in Command

> **(a) The Pilot in command of an aircraft is
> directly responsible for, and is the
> final authority as to, the operation
> of that aircraft.**

1

Flying—How Difficult Is It?

FLYING APPEARS to be complicated. It seems that way because of the depth of its theory, the complexity of the vehicle, the capriciousness of the element it works in, and the aiming it takes to have the airplane arrive where it is supposed to.

Yet how can anything that has its classic beauty be difficult? The graceful motions and cleanness of form make it appear as a unity of faultless action.

Dig deep into the magic art of flying and it can be complicated—the theories and study of aerodynamics, even the question of air flow over a wing, alone, can fill a book and leave much unanswered.

The machinery of the airplane—systems, electronics and all the stuff commonly known as the nuts and bolts of the business—is extensive and encumbered.

The weather, an unfathomable surprise element, is never understood completely. Its effects on an airplane can be discussed for long periods—and an element of awe often lurks in the background.

Navigation in this vehicle that has no bounds and can subtly slide off in any direction is not simple, although the magic of technology has taken it from an esoteric art to a matter of facts, figures and computer programming; the pilot needs only to push a few buttons, tune a radio and "follow the needle" that gets the airplane where it should go. Of course a good pilot knows certain essentials, because even the most sophisticated gadget will, on occasion, fail; then knowledge of the art is needed. And knowing the art is useful so that one can periodically cast a questioning eye on the fancy gadgetry—watching where the compass tells us we're headed is never a bad idea.

Difficult?

So flying is difficult and complicated. No! It really is not. There are essentials that once known will bring a quality that makes the remainder automatic. With these essentials firmly in mind new things are quickly understood, put in proper category and the fears coming from them made barren.

It is an impossible task to know all, but is it necessary? There are expert airmen who fly for a lifetime and never know much about flying in its complicated form. I knew such a pilot who had two of the four engines fail right after takeoff in a Lockheed Constellation. He staggered around the field on a hot Kansas day, going under a bridge in the process, and landed back at the airport safely. In the investigation the government inspector said that theoretically it was impossible! But he didn't reckon on how well that pilot knew the feather edge between flying and falling.

People like that are knowledgeable on certain basics that protect them from all comers—they know fundamentals, tricks of the trade, and have a bag full of right and wrong things to do or not to do that they put together by experience, study and crafty observation. These are the smart fliers, and they do smart flying.

Simple?

After a lifetime of flying I am convinced that it is simple art, and nature meant it that way. I do not find myself, when I fly, with a head full of facts and theories. The essentials have been part of my flying life; I don't think of them; they just happen, and they take care of the rest automatically. This isn't to say I don't have an interesting time trying to put theory and what I see and experience together, but in the rush of a busy time the essentials take care of me without thought.

In the beginning, of course, one must learn and be conscious of principles and procedures—think about them. This, then, says we go slowly at first, making certain we're doing the right thing. If a situation is more complicated than we can handle or it's moving faster than we can think about it, then we back off—turn around, land, don't go, or whatever. As experience is gained we can move into deeper areas, do it right automatically *if* we've learned the basics—the simple basics.

That's what we're going to attempt to do here—point out basics and explain key things that get people in trouble or keep them out of it.

2

Using Controls

AN AIRPLANE, or glider, resting on the ground, immobile, but graceful in form, is often talked about as an animate object, somehow possessed of a soul and capable of inspiring flight within itself.

All good stuff for poets and romantics—and who hasn't been either at some time or another. But let's face hard facts; an aircraft, empty of humans, on the ground alone, no matter how beautiful, is simply a bunch of metal, wood, rubber, fiberglass or whatever, and if you took it all apart and piled the pieces it would be just a pile of pieces.

The aircraft on its own can do nothing; its natural tendency, if left to itself in the air, is eventually to get in a spiral dive and reach the earth in a clumsy manner.

Contrary to this cruel but realistic look at an aircraft is the wonder of its capability: to go high and fast, to combat weather, to fly over far, remote, merciless terrain and do it with a certain disdain. It can do these things as a result of the genius of those who designed and created it.

Of course it needs one more important thing—a pilot to fly it. Aircraft do appear to have souls, but the souls they have are a harmony of their capabilities and the pilot's skill. When a pilot takes controls in hand the aircraft then becomes the living thing we romanticize about.

[6]

How the aircraft performs, what sort of character it demonstrates, depends on the manner in which the pilot moves its controls. He or she can obtain the ultimate performance designed into the aircraft, or do very badly by it.

So, fundamental to it all, the beginning, the foundation, is how one moves the controls. Yes, the basic matter of how hands and feet rest on and move stick, wheel, pedals and levers. They should rest lightly and use persuasive, gentle pressures.

The jargon of flight is contrary to good control manipulation. We talk of "kicking" rudder, "shoving over," "hauling back" and other harsh terms when in actuality a good pilot does none of these things.

How these expressions do harm was demonstrated to me by a close friend. He had been around me and my flying friends for many hangar sessions, listening with interest to our extravagant tales of adventure, although he knew little of flying. He asked if I'd give him some flight instruction.

Once aloft I gave him the controls. Shortly the airplane lurched and skidded to the right—it startled me.

"Gad man! What are you doing?" I shouted.

"The nose started off so I kicked rudder."

He had heard us talk about "kicking" rudder, and that's what he did—slammed his foot on the rudder pedal!

All the good pilots I have flown with are very delicate handling controls; they use pressures, and their action is almost imperceptible; even those times when large control movements are needed there is a smooth, unjerky way they make the moves.

Flying a good instrument approach is like safecracking in its delicateness. Watch Gilbert Defer, Concord test pilot with whom I flew the Concord simulator.

We were making ILS approaches and doing them with control augmentation off, which means you are essentially making direct control inputs to the airplane without any computer gadgetry to help overcome the difficult low-speed control characteristics of a

delta wing when you are trying to fly a precise airspeed down a
glide slope.

I asked Defer to do one before I tried it. The approach was
made at 165 knots. We came down the ILS glued to the center; we
never varied from being on course, and the indicated airspeed sat
exactly on 165 knots. What made it especially interesting was that
the movement of Defer's hands was almost indiscernible, just a
suggestion of motion—a masterful job by a master.

I talked to him about it and complimented him on his smoothness and excellent work.

"It is pressures, little pressures, no more," he said.

That's what it is, putting on pressure and taking it off—enough
to feel that the aircraft is responding quietly and promptly.

3

Feet, Too

FEET ARE an important part of using controls, although there seems to be a tendency to use feet less, and that should not be.

Feet control the rudder pedals and, as part of them, the wheel brakes. Let's talk about the rudder first. More and more I hear the rudder referred to as the "rudders." I don't know when that got started because most airplanes have one rudder; perhaps it's a reference to the pedals and not the rudder. Small stuff, and what pilots call it-them is unimportant *as long as they use it-them.*

Where one uses rudder:

During taxi. (This includes nose- or tail-wheel steering.)

During the takeoff run, to keep the airplane straight down the runway.

During the takeoff run to keep it straight if an engine—on multiengine airplanes—fails.

During flight to keep the airplane straight with an engine out.

During stall maneuvers to maintain a heading while slowing and approaching stall. (No time to be messing with ailerons.)

During the time we slip an airplane on landing approach.

During rough air to keep the tail from swinging.

Last, and not least by any means, starting and stopping turns.

The last one is the basic we all know about: We want to turn, we lower a wing with ailerons, the drag of the upwing aileron wants to keep the airplane going straight so we put a little pressure on the rudder in the direction of turn and overcome the negative or adverse yaw—voila! The turn is under way. That's called coordination.

The opposite occurs when stopping a turn.

Now if we didn't touch the rudder the power of the wing—the lift vector—would eventually get the airplane turning. It would be a sloppy entry with a noticeable unpleasant, skidding feeling unless one is an insensible kluck. There seem to be a lot of insensible klucks around.

The longer, straighter the wing is, the more pronounced the negative yaw characteristic—glider pilots never feel there's enough rudder on long-wing sailplanes. Sweptwing airline-type airplanes seem to have less negative yaw. This can be attributed to various things: use of spoilers on the down wing to help the aileron and cause some drag; shorter span; and gadgetry in the control systems of hydraulic, gyro and electronic nature. Airline pilots don't use their feet much when making turns in the sweptwing jets. They tend to forget how to use their feet.

As we said, gliders need lots of rudder input, so one uses his or her feet. I was checking out, in a sailplane, a friend who was a 747 captain but hadn't flown much except airline airplanes for many years. He had a terrible time trying to coordinate turns in that sailplane and even keeping it straight on tow when coordinated turns were needed. I didn't turn him loose, but left it up to an instructor with more patience.

Today's airplanes have been designed to keep negative yaw to a minimum, and a good job has been done—but this tends to have people use their feet less, although there's still sloppiness in turn starts and stops. The trend not to use rudder makes sloppy pilots. It can also make passengers sick.

The DC-2 and DC-3 swung their tails in rough air, a wild swishing back and forth that made passengers very ill. A good pilot could minimize the effect by fighting the tail swinging with his feet. There was a trick to getting opposite rudder in, just at the right time or one could aggravate the situation. One tried to push the rudder in the direction the nose was swinging just as it reached the peak of the swing and before it started the other way—if the nose swung right, right rudder was applied at the peak of the swing and then released slowly. It was constant, hard work. Lazy pilots wouldn't expend the effort; they just let the passengers suffer. As a copilot I noticed that the pilots who used the rudder were smoother, better pilots. When I became a captain it was woe unto the copilot who didn't try to reduce tail swinging when he flew! "Use your feet!" was an outburst of mine that probably didn't win me any popularity prizes, but the passenger's comfort is important, and aside from that, sloppy flying just grates on my nerves. I often have to bite my tongue when flying with a pilot in his own airplane who doesn't use rudder and just lets it wallow about the sky. I only fly with that kind once.

Pilots in today's jets don't have to fight the tail swinging business because the airplanes are all equipped with yaw dampers that do the job for them—some light twins and sophisticated singles have them too. These are part of the hydraulic, gyro, electronic system of the airplane. Without them a jet would be as bad, or worse, than a DC-3.

Dutch Roll

It's a phenomenon of sweptwings called Dutch Roll—yaw-roll coupling in fancier terms—in which the airplane lowers a wing, the tail swings, the wing bottoms out, then rises, and the tail swings the other way. It's a kind of corkscrew motion that keeps repeating during a period of about seven seconds—at least that's the way the 707 was. The later jets like the 747 have better characteristics, and the latest, such as the 767, are even better—they also have less sweep than previous airline jets. Without a yaw damper they would be pretty wild and a lot of work to control, so the yaw damper was put on for that reason and not just to make less work for pilots.

A well coordinated turn is part of the beauty of flight, part of that smooth feeling of exhilaration the freedom of flying gives one. But aside from this esthetic value, using rudder well in turns teaches one the feel when needed—engines out, slips and all those things.

Wheel Brakes

While we're talking feet and rudder pedals we might as well mention brakes. Heavy feet make for jerky braking, annoying to passengers, wearing on tires and brakes, which cost money. Brakes should be used only as needed and not as something to ride. The most pathetic bit of brake use is when one sees a pilot taxiing with a lot of power, kicking up dust and noise while using brakes to keep from going too fast! Also, locking one wheel with a brake while bursting the engine to a state of wild confusion as he or she tries to turn the airplane on the ground. Let the inside wheel rotate a tiny bit and the turn goes much easier.

Brakes are overused. Dwane Wallace, the man who built the Cessna Company from the beginning and for years was its board chairman, a superb pilot, says, "Brakes should be thought of as an emergency device and treated that way." A sage piece of advice.

Anticipation and gentle proper pressures as needed get the job done. A particularly annoying brake application is when the airplane is being parked. A simple trick makes the stop smooth and without that lurch as the airplane—automobiles too—comes to a stop. The trick is to release brake pressure—let up on the feet's pushing—just as the airplane comes to rest. When I was a child and trolley cars were still around I often stood, fascinated, near the conductor as he turned a big handle to make the car go or slow and stop. They had it down pat, and I can remember how just as the trolley slowed to a stop he'd turn that big handle toward off and release all arresting pressure. The stop would be smooth as glass, and standing passengers wouldn't be heaved around.

Feet, like hands, require pressures, pressures on and off, made gently and only in amounts needed on flight controls or brakes. They should be used, and practice and awareness soon makes their use automatic.

4

Feel

FEEL IS MORE than one thing; it's a sense of acceleration and deceleration on our body—that's called seat-of-the-pants flying; it's a sense of the feel of the control pressures; it's a sense of noise level; it's certain visual cues. All these make up what's called feel.

Feel is an essential part of flying; good pilots have developed it to a fine degree. But we don't fly by feel alone; it isn't quantitative; it doesn't give precise information; in the final analysis we must have a combination of feel, technical knowledge and instruments. What feel really does is provide us cues that tell us to check our condition by instruments and any other methods available.

Aside from feel in the sense of acceleration on one's body, there's a sense of feel of the airplane and its controls, of when controls are firm and the airplane flying well, or when they are "soft" and the airplane is flying perhaps too slowly, when a heaviness of elevator control develops in a tight turn or pull-up. All these tell a pilot how the airplane is flying, and the more such a sense is developed the better the pilot. Observation and slow flight practice improve these aspects of feel.

I remember, vividly, when I developed an awareness of feel over fifty years ago. I had recently acquired a Pitcairn Mailwing biplane; open cockpit, 220 horsepower Wright J-5, the type airplane Eastern Air Transport was flying mail with. My total flying time was about seventy-five hours, and I didn't know much. My landing approaches were made with excess speed, and I floated across the airport allowing precious ground to go by under me that I should have been on.

Johnny Pumyea was a veteran pilot who came by the airport from time to time: World War I, Air Mail, barnstorming were all in his log book, and we neophytes looked upon him with awe. Somehow, the reason lost in time, I took a ride as passenger in my airplane, with Pumyea flying it. We approached for a landing, but it felt very different from my landing approaches. It wasn't the fast glide; instead there was a certain feeling of the nose being higher, of slowness, of docility—but also of everything being perfectly under control—and of airspeed that I had never felt before. The impression was so strong it got me in a high pitch of excitement, and I couldn't wait to fly the airplane myself. I'd felt the art of flying.

We landed. Pumyea got out, and I climbed in the back cockpit, taxied out and took off. Flying felt different; the climb seemed more positive. At altitude I tried glides—slower glides. I slowed them to stall and found I still had a good margin between glide and stall. Then I approached for landing—slower than ever before, but I could "feel" the airplane. Though settling, the airplane was flying well, and I knew where it was flying. I made a good landing, far shorter than ever before. I had flown the airplane; before I had been driving it. Pumyea showed me, without saying a word, that speed was delicate, it was harmful on both ends, that too much had as serious faults as too little. That you used it with skill and judgment, and adding speed just to be safer wasn't a panacea.

Speed

The art and skill of speed is in using the minimum that contains a speed buffer to protect against prevailing conditions, but not so much that an airplane becomes jumpy, that the delicacy of flying is lost in the confusion of excess speed and tight controls and that nothing connects you with the feel of the airplane. This isn't stall protection—the feel of approach to stall is hidden in the disarray of too much speed—and we haven't mentioned the increased hazard of overshooting the runway, with its implications.

The proper speed, of course, is a computed reference speed: stall plus 30 percent generally, with a proper gust factor added, such as half the gust velocity. We knew nothing of this in Pitcairn days.

q

Noise is part of feel. One can sense the noise and its relationship to what the airplane's condition is.

Air rushing at the airplane and hitting it head on is called q, which is the symbol for dynamic pressure. Technical pilots talk about q noise when the noise due to speed is high. It changes with altitude-density. The noise of a Boeing 727 is very loud when going fast at low altitude, but subsides to a whisper at the same speed at high altitude—the difference in q.

The air flow, q, in a sense, is speed, so if the noise is high we're doing well; if the noise is low we may be getting too slow.

The slicker the airplane—the farther the engines from the cockpit as with the aft-mounted engines on jet airplanes—the quieter the airplane becomes and the less recognizable q noise is, so one has to rely more on the other senses of feel. But even the slickest airplane has changing noise values; they are most subtle, but they are still useful. But one should be warned that quiet, clean modern airplanes have less and less cues available from noise, and the other feel values become the important ones.

There is a feel of the airplane that develops from what one sees. For example, near the ground on landing: A high sink rate develops; our eyes will sense this just from the way the ground begins to move toward us faster. This can happen in a Cessna 150 or a Boeing 747.

Visual "feel" can be negative too. We make a downwind turn near the ground; the visual cue of the ground rushing by makes us feel we're going very fast, which may be true in ground speed, but our airspeed may be low, and any attempt to go slower, by visual cues, can result in a stall. So while we can feel by visual cues, we must, as in all feel, refer back to instruments before we act.

But basically we're talking about feel as it relates to acceleration on our body, control feel and noise.

We don't mean to give the impression that feel is the best way to fly an airplane. What we're trying to say is that good pilots use feel as part of their total flying ability. The best way to fly is to know what the instruments are telling us and then use them, but feel is a cue to let us know that things aren't as they should be and we'd better look around carefully at instruments.

We said feel wasn't quantitative, but rather a cue that tells us to look at instruments and see what's going on—find the quantity. This is true except that as experience grows and feel becomes more sensitive a pilot naturally will not always wait to move controls until looking at instruments. If, for example, controls become soft and noise drops off it's a cue we're getting slow. The experienced pilot will be pushing ahead some toward getting more speed as his eyes travel toward the airspeed indicator and the attitude. This is fine stuff, but not the paramount factor—number one is the quantitative information instruments give us.

Simulator Feel

The fact that the cues of feel are important is demonstrated by the very sophisticated simulators used for flight training. They have motion of some sort or another. A modern simulator has the cockpit cab mounted on a structure of hydraulically controlled legs that moves the entire cab in order to give some sort of feel to those flying.

These motion cues, as hard as they try to make them realistic, and as expensive as they are, don't precisely reproduce feel—at times you feel as though you are just being jerked around.

There's been a lot of effort to improve simulator feel, and I've seen and flown some pretty weird stuff experimentally. At NASA's Ames Laboratory I flew an SST simulator, in the SST's early stages, that had a small cab mounted on a long arm, maybe thirty feet long, that could swing like a centrifuge. The cab was also mounted on gimbals, and you could go upside-down and be slung around until you were sick. It was for the purpose of studying handling qualities and control during engine cuts at Mach 3 and things of that nature. But they wanted feel—even in an SST.

I also saw a trial motion system that was a vertical track, the height of a hangar, mounted on the outside of a hangar, so the cab went up and down to give the feel of acceleration and deceleration.

Simulators duplicate control pressures exactly; they load up or get light just as the real airplane does. Even noise is simulated. So you can see that even though using instruments is the basis, feel is still recognized as an important part of flying.

We need feel and we need control, but then we must have information with which to direct the airplane, and this brings us to another first-order fundamental, closely linked to and as important as handling the controls. It is scan.

5

About Scan

IF ONE'S SCAN is good then the airplane will never get far off the intended path or attitude and one will not be duped into big, jerky, rough control movements. Good scan means good control quality—one complements the other.

Scan means to look around, but it means to look quickly and with purpose. Saying *quickly* isn't meant to give an impression of darting, frantic motion; rather it means looking at something—instrument or whatever—long enough to register what it is showing and then getting on to the next thing. Quickness means not to linger unnecessarily and develop a fixation on one thing while neglecting others. One may stare at the ILS cross pointer and not notice the horizon in time to catch a pitch or wing-level change that's developed. When we finally wake up and look at attitude the aircraft has gotten far enough off to require a big control movement to get back. And big corrections are things to avoid, because they are difficult to keep smooth and they tend to cause overshoots in the opposite direction that require more large-control movement, and the thing gets to be a mess.

Research on scanning and what a pilot sees has gone on for a long time by NASA, the FAA, the U.S. Air Force and the U.S. Navy, universities, organizations and individuals. Today, at NASA, this research has reached a high level of sophistication.

The big help in this work has been a device known as an oculo-meter that uses infrared light to reflect from an eye's cornea. The reflection is computerized, and from this is determined what a pilot looks at and for how long. The device is so precise it can measure eye movement within half a degree—about the size of a dime on the instrument panel—and do it thirty times a second!

The research has shown that the ADI (attitude direction indi-cator, which is a fancy name for artificial horizon) is the instru-ment looked at most. This solidly backs up the truth that if the airplane's attitude is kept proper the airplane will never be far from where one wants it, provided the power is reasonable and the air speed fairly stabilized. *This is a basic key in flying—IFR or VFR.*

The time spent looking at each instrument—dwell time, they call it—shows that one doesn't tarry long on one instrument. The ADI, the instrument looked at most, was only "dwelled" on for two thirds of a second to a second and a half at a time.

It was found that a scan isn't a circular motion in which one starts at one corner, goes around the panel and winds up back at the beginning corner again. Rather it's a recognition that the ADI—the instrument or the real horizon—is where the basic in-formation is for what's going on. We give more time to that and then go to other instruments as needed, then quickly back to the ADI. There doesn't seem to be a "best" pattern, but the ADI is the center of attention.

It was also found that distractions change the scan and cause dwell time to increase. A distracting voice may cause a pilot to freeze during the scan, causing a dwell time of as much as ten to fifteen seconds on one instrument, which is a long, long time. The times decrease with experience, and experienced pilots can stand distractions better. These pilots have learned time-share looking, which may be one reason they can cope with complex situations better than the neophyte pilot.

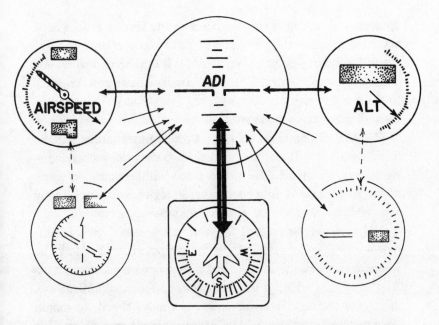

The scan pattern: The ADI is the focus and the eye makes quick trips out to other instruments and back to the ADI. Now and then it may go from one instrument to another before going back to the ADI, but this isn't predominant. The ADI is the thing because it says what the airplane's attitude is, which, with a quick reference to other instruments, says where we are and where we're likely to be going—attitude is the key and that's the ADI.

Basic T

The Basic T arrangement of the flying instruments was developed during the early days of instrument flying and came into general use about 1946. It recognized the importance of attitude—artificial horizon—and put it as the central instrument.

The Basic T has the ADI in the center of the *T*s horizontal; to the right is the altimeter and to the left, indicated air speed. Just below the ADI, on the *T*s vertical, is the directional information—HSI or directional gyro.

This concept has withstood the test of time, and all serious instrument aircraft, including the latest airline aircraft with cathode ray tube instrument presentations, have them arranged in the Basic T pattern. One might say the ADI is the hub of a wheel and the scan pattern goes out the spokes to other instruments, but back to the hub the major portion of time. The Basic T is an arrangement to make this action natural.

The ADI is important because, as we've said, attitude is the thing we fly by. If our attitude says a wing is down we know we're turning. If the nose is down we will probably be going down; if the nose is up we are either going up or we're slowing and need power or a lower nose before we get too slow.

Adding power or pushing the nose down comes from an attitude that demands action, but before any action we have to know where the nose is, the attitude, and that comes from looking at the ADI or, flying VFR, at the real horizon. The real horizon, out there over the nose, is as important as the ADI, and we should learn to use it as well as the ADI, because when we're flying VFR we should be looking out, not in, except for quick looks. Pilots use instruments in the airplane as their main cues for flight, but any good pilot can do the necessary attitude flying looking outside too. So when we talk about attitude we generally mean ADI inside and horizon outside as the same thing.

When we fly a heading, be it cross-country or down an ILS, attitude is the key. The gyro or compass tells one a number; it doesn't say a thing about how the airplane is flying except for the way it's tracking or if it's turning. What says where it's going is the pitch and roll attitude. The heading is 220°, and we want to change it to 280°. Where do we look? What do we do? We lower a wing; the horizon tells us how much we've lowered it, and that's an indication of how fast we'll turn. As the heading approaches the one we want the wings are leveled, and the turn is stopped. (Let's not get nitpicky about rudder and negative yaw and all that—stick the wing down and we'll turn, finally, negative yaw or not.)

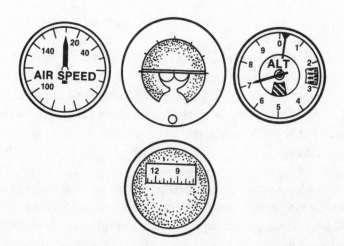

The Basic T: It has proved itself for 40 years. What it really demonstrates is the fact that attitude—ADI—is the dominant instrument, the starting point for information to tell how we are doing or will do.

The top drawing shows how the Basic T started with artificial horizon and directional gyro; the lower picture is typical of the setup in a Boeing 767, and shows how the Basic T is still there, even with the modern cathode ray tube instruments.

Or we want to fly in steady state—to hold altitude, hold a heading and bore through the sky like an arrow. How? Look at the ADI. If a wing isn't down—unless we're trimmed in some awful manner—the airplane is going straight. Nose on the proper point and we'll be flying near level, on the altitude we want. Air movement and required power changes will alter that a bit, but basically if the pitch is where we want it the other factors will be smallish and most certainly second in line. So one looks at attitude as the primary point of focus before anything else is done. Without attitude information—pitch and roll—we don't have a reference to start from.

Scanning is important. We've seen that the center of the scan is the ADI; we've seen that distractions can disrupt the scanning process, but that experienced pilots are bothered less than inexperienced ones; that fixation on an instrument for an excessive length of time removes the value of scanning. Neophyte pilots, when doubt arises or distractions occur, tend to stare. The key is to keep scanning, and if there's any doubt about where to look first, look at the ADI but don't stare at it. It seems that anything over three seconds is bordering on staring.

6

What Other Instruments Say

THERE ARE information instruments used in conjunction with the attitude instruments. They are airspeed indicator, vertical speed indicator and heading information.

Airspeed Indicator

Let's take the airspeed indicator first. What does it do? Two things; one is to tell a number. We can take that number, apply temperature and altitude and get true airspeed for navigation and performance information. We can also look at an airspeed number and get an indication of how close to stall we are, or if our approach speed is correct, or climb—a number of useful things.

Aside from the information numbers, however, the airspeed indicator is an acceleration instrument. It tells how the airplane is accelerating or decelerating.

Lag

Often one hears about airspeed lag. Well, it's hogwash. No such thing. What's lagging is the airplane, and the airspeed indicator reflects this. An airspeed indicator is a pressure differential instrument that collects total pressure—what's being shoved against the airplane—and static pressure, the pressure of the air around us. From these two pressures it computes and reads out airspeed. The total pressure comes via the pitot tube that got its name from a Frenchman, Henri Pitot, who invented the idea in 1732 while trying to measure the speed of water flowing near the bottom of the River Seine—nothing's new.

It's pretty obvious that the pressure that changes airspeed doesn't take very long to register. There's a little lag because of friction and so on, but it's so tiny, probably around a tenth of a second, that we don't notice it in the sense people talk of airspeed lag.

The airspeed *seems* to lag because the airplane is changing its state and it takes time to do it. You cannot fly 150 knots one moment and 250 knots the next instant!

Example: We're nose high, very slow, we push the nose down to gain speed. (Power enters this too, but there are times power isn't enough. The relationship between power and airspeed will unnecessarily complicate our example. After all there's no power in a glider, and we get the job done. There are times when the nose has to be moved to increase or decrease airspeed and power be damned!)

So we've pushed the nose down and speed begins to increase, slowly at first, but quickly as we accelerate. The airspeed indicator reflects this; it begins to show a speed increase slowly and then the indicating needle moves faster toward a higher speed; if we don't pull back we'll build lots of speed. Now, importantly, the rate the airspeed indicator needle is moving tells us how fast we're accelerating and how to pull back so the speed will not dive to big numbers. The airspeed needle by its rate of movement tells us acceleration—not *g*'s in the sense of load, but *rate* of acceleration. The movement, incidentally, also tells dive angle.

Experience tells us how to push or pull to get the airspeed we want by recognizing the rate of movement of the airspeed indi-

Left to right: Changing nose doesn't change airspeed until the airplane has had a chance to accelerate, and then the airspeed increases at an increasing rate, as shown in airplane at far right. The airspeed indicator's action is a cue that the nose is pretty far down, or you wouldn't be accelerating so fast. Obviously this works in the opposite direction too—going from nose down at high speed, to nose up; it takes a while for the speed to decrease—decelerate—and the nose may be quite high before you see much speed decrease on the airspeed indicator.

cation. Little rate movement and little pressures are necessary; big rate movement and stronger, but careful, pressures are used. If the airspeed indicator is wildly accelerating toward a high number we don't want to haul back hard; we have to use positive, steady, strong but careful pressures—or we might bend the wings. (Any idiot, in this case, would have power off!)

Of course, attitude enters this. If the nose is way down and the airspeed building up, we know it's going to build up even faster—so we have to get the nose up. Conversely, if the nose is well up and the speed slowing, that nose has to come down.

All this is saying that the airspeed indicator's information on rate can be nicely combined with attitude to tell how much control pressure is needed to get on the airspeed desired and do it *smoothly* and without overshoots.

Sounds like simple stuff to pilots with thousands of hours who know all this by experience and do it automatically. They are smooth pilots. But there are some who, despite thousands of hours, are rough, and one feels it riding in their airplane. It's inexcusable to be rough. It isn't just a matter of being smooth for smoothness' sake alone, but smoothness also means a pilot who has it all together, who anticipates and is leading the action, not stumbling along behind it. Thinking about the information that instruments can give beyond just telling a number can do a lot toward making a smooth pilot.

Vertical Speed

The vertical speed indicator (VSI) is another rate instrument that can show acceleration as well as values. The vertical speed indicator does have lag, in the order of four seconds. That doesn't mean it takes four seconds to begin to move; no, it begins to move almost instantly after the airplane has changed its direction or rate—this is very helpful in level flight, especially in smooth air, because this first movement is a cue that the airplane is beginning to move in that direction. It takes four seconds to settle on a new number after the airplane reaches a steady state, but the first movement is a very useful signal.

So if we're juggling stick and/or power frequently, the vertical speed will be moving a lot—it does in the unevenness of rough air too. But despite its fidgety ways it's useful if used sensibly with the airspeed indicator.

Indicated airspeed increasing and the vertical speed showing an increasing descent rate say you're going down, with the trend toward going down even faster.

If airspeed is decreasing and the vertical speed shows an increasing rate of climb, you're going up, but the cue is that this climb isn't going to go on forever and may end soon. The moment the vertical speed reverses and starts to show descent, with airspeed still slowing, you can be certain you are in stall territory and it's time to do something about it!

The vertical speed indicator, with its lag, is an inexact type indication, but if one learns its actions and interrelationships with the airspeed indicator, it can be a valuable tool. One should learn to use it, because during level flight and instrument approaches it's very useful indeed—and more about that later on. (There are vertical speed indicators available with almost no lag, but they are

expensive and found on airline and corporate jet aircraft—a really
great and useful instrument.)

Altimeter

The sensitive altimeter also shows something beyond a number
to read—like 5,000 feet. Because it is sensitive, the hundreds-of-
feet needle moves in large enough amounts to be seen even
though the airplane has only climbed or descended twenty feet or
so. So one can detect a climb or descent almost the instant it
starts. During steep turns—especially when we're being checked
and trying to hold exact altitude and impress the check pilot, or
during a circle to land under a low ceiling—there's often excessive concentration on the altimeter to be certain we're staying on
altitude. As we're doing this a movement of the sensitive
hundred-foot hand, even twenty feet, is an immediate warning
that we're letting the nose drop or the bank steepen—that we've
forgotten to keep our scan of instruments going and we'd better
check attitude and any other instruments required.

Therefore, while the vertical speed indicator and altimeter are
not basically for the purpose, they can give cues that loudly say
we'd better check back to the ADI or HSI (Horizontal Situation
Indicator). It's a matter of other instruments being useful in giving hints as to what diversions may be starting. (Diversions are
generally called excursions in the trade.)

Heading

Even our heading information is useful as a cue instrument;
we're in a turn and checking the heading to see how far we are
from the heading we want to stop on, but while looking we notice
the heading is changing faster. It's an immediate signal that we're
steepening the bank, and we'd better check the ADI.

Almost all flight instruments are related, and what each can do, outside its basic function such as telling altitude in the case of the altimeter, is important because it makes instrument flying, or contact, easier and smoother. All the subtle cues properly recognized and used forestall large excursions and help us keep the airplane tightly within the bounds we want it.

If one scans properly and has a knowledge of all the cues instruments can give, the airplane flies where one wants it, with small control pressures and minimum wanderings from the desired path. Flight then is smoothly done, and this smoothness creates a quietude that in turn gives a relaxed and confident feeling to the pilot that further makes his judgment and actions unemotional and well thought out.

One may feel we harp on smoothness, but there's good reason for it, and a long time flying and checking hundreds of pilots fortifies the fact that smooth pilots are better pilots—safer and more efficient.

To say it again about scanning: The key instrument is the ADI—artificial or real horizon. The other instruments are necessary, but ancillary.

7

The Wing, Air and Alpha

A MOST FUNDAMENTAL fact is that there has to be smooth air flowing over the wing in order to fly. The delicate feel and knowledge of this action must, somehow, be in a pilot's bag of tricks.

There are different ways of knowing; we can get esoteric and delve into laminar flow, separated flow, boundary layer, density and a host of related things; or we can learn it by "feel" with an understanding of what the aircraft's instruments tell us, along with a few, but necessary, basic facts. Let's try that route.

Alpha

The most important block to place under our foundation of knowledge is the wing we fly on and what it can and cannot do. There's no use getting too complicated except to mention a few key points, and one of them is angle of attack, or alpha as it's referred to, using the symbol α.

The definition of angle of attack, if we want to be pedantic, is the angle between the relative wind and the wing cord. What tells or shows us that? Ah, here's the rub. You don't see it unless you have an angle-of-attack indicator and only a tiny percentage of the airplanes flying have such an instrument.

Now some may argue that the stall warning is an angle of attack indicator, but it isn't. It just tells when one is approaching the critical angle of attack by a buzzer, whistle or gadget that shakes the stick called a Stick Shaker—although most airplanes have control wheels. The tricky part of all this is the relative wind. It's not the head-on wind, but the wind coming at the airplane in a fashion best described by an example:

Visualize an airplane flying in level attitude at low or insufficient power. The horizon bar—pitch attitude—may show a few degrees nose up, but the angle of attack might be as high as $14°$ since the relative wind is flowing up toward the wing because the airplane is mushing—another word for settling. So we have a pitch angle of, say, $3°$ but the angle of attack is $14°$.

What does all this mean to us flying the airplane? Not much except for one very important point: We can stall with the nose up, down or sideways, so that just looking ahead to see where the nose is on the horizon, real or artificial, is not any guarantee that we will know if the angle of attack, at that moment, is near stall. In other words, pitch attitude—nose position vis-à-vis the horizon—isn't the same as angle of attack except in some coincidental cases that we don't concern ourselves with.

A wing stalls at a certain angle of attack. It doesn't matter if the airplane is heavy, light, fast, slow or whatever; if the angle exceeds the stall angle the wing will cease lifting enough to be of any use, and most airplanes, if continued in that condition, that is, holding full up elevator, will spin. This stall angle is around $16°$ for wings shaped in the ordinary manner that don't have considerable sweep. The $16°$ varies from airfoil to airfoil by a few degrees. The value isn't important—on most airplanes we can't read it anyway.

What we're really interested in is what tells us when the wing is being flown at high angle and we'd best be careful. Some of this knowledge comes from what we see—large pitch angle and slow speed means the alpha is high, but it can be subtle because a lowish pitch angle and slow speed can result in a fairly high alpha also. (We're going to call angle of attack by its name, alpha, from here on because it's less to write and we can sound like test pilots when they talk because they always refer to it that way.)

Drag

Interesting to all this is the snowball effect of alpha. As alpha increases so does drag. Up to 6°, roughly, the drag increases slowly, but after that, toward stall alpha, the drag rises quickly. Lift increases at higher angles—if the wing isn't stalled. But lift isn't free, and an important point to remember is that we pay for lift by drag. You don't get something for nothing, and this is especially true with lift. So as alpha becomes higher, lift increases, but so does drag until the stall alpha, when it all goes to pot, and there's far more drag than lift and the smooth flow over the wing burbles and tumbles—even reverses. The wing stops lifting. The disturbed air occurs not all at once but in progression. What happens is that as we slow and approach higher alpha, air begins to burble and break away from the wing, just toward the trailing edge at first; mostly this adds drag, but a little more increase in alpha and there's more disturbed air flow and more drag. Then the process, as we further increase alpha, begins to gain momentum until the air flow over the wing separates, and we're finished flying; how fast it progresses depends on how fast alpha is increasing—or crudely, how hard one is hauling back on stick or wheel.

The disturbed, mixed-up air over the wing that kills its lifting ability is important to remember, and we'll talk about it later.

We should talk about altitude too because high altitude flying, jet or prop, means we are running out of power. The airplane is power limited. So if we are struggling to accelerate when our speed is low, alpha can, sneakily, get high. Manhandling or

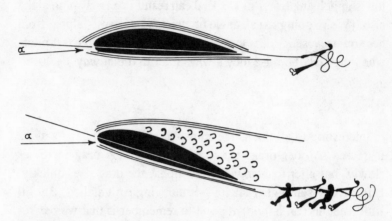

The wing with smooth flow and disturbed flow. Higher alpha on bottom drawing
shows flow separation and drag increase. Airplane mushes downward. The wing
is about stalled. It's necessary to lower the leading edge of the wing to reduce
alpha and have flow change from separated to smooth, as in top drawing. If alpha isn't reduced, adding power will not cure the problem. The wing has to be
clean before the power will be useful. Get the nose down! The actions—nose
down and power application—can be close together or simultaneous, but the
key is that alpha must be reduced!

trying to force the airplane higher can be trouble, turbulence can
be trouble, a fast turn is a prelude to a quick spin. The air is thin,
the power is low, and it's a place to be careful and aware.

So where are we? What does this mean to one flying an airplane? You don't see alpha, there are few airplanes with an alpha
instrument, the pitch attitude isn't the same as alpha except
in some cases that we couldn't possibly sort out, and how many
degrees bring on stall is just nice information, but useless as we
fly.

We have to have a way to fly to keep us from stalling, to help
us fly the right speeds on approach, climb and all the rest that will
not get us in dangerous alpha territory. And we don't want to be
thinking about it when there are many other things to think about.

In the airplane we have indicated airspeed and attitude. When we are flying level, straight ahead, no bank, not accelerating or decelerating (called steady state in test-pilot lingo), airspeed tells where we are in relation to stall (one of the few instances alpha and pitch are very nearly the same). So airspeed takes the place of an alpha instrument? No! It doesn't because g's, acceleration in relation to gravity, get in the act. G's acting on the airplane above a value of one mean the airplane effectively weighs more, so that it takes a *higher airspeed to keep from the stall alpha.*

Where do we find extra g's in most normal flight? In turns. So while the airplane stalls at a certain airspeed straight and level steady state, it stalls at a higher one in turns, and the steeper the turn the higher the speed. So now we know that to protect us from stall we need to be aware of speed and anything that's causing g's—turns, sharp pull-ups and gusty air.

Shear gets in the act, but it's different, and we'll talk about it later.

So, really, if we keep airspeed sufficient for the situation we are flying we'll not exceed stall alpha—situation meaning straight ahead level, climb, glide or anything that increases the g load, mostly turns. Why do pilots spin in while circling their girl friend's house? Steep turn, trying to stay over the house, perhaps looking back and unconsciously pulling the stick back farther, inattention to how the airplane's flying, increased g loads and low speed. Cross controls get in this act too, but let's stick to getting too slow, because if the speed is sufficient most modern airplanes can take a little mishandling and be forgiving. But don't mishandle while also going too slow. That's very bad news.

Inattention is a big cause. Lack of scanning. Quick looks at attitude and airspeed would prevent all this. Feel does too if you have a sense of it. The airplane begins to respond sloppily; there's an uncomfortable squashy feeling in the seat of one's pants. In a steep turn the elevator gets heavier, and we need more back pressure to keep the turn where we want it; it's time to look around and see where the airspeed is and the attitude—ADI or horizon.

But put it together; too slow a speed means high alpha; too many *g*'s such as in turns means high alpha. How to prevent these things? Know about them first, then don't dope off! Attention, scan. Know where the airspeed is and what the attitude is. Actually it's all very simple.

8

So We Stall or Spin

THE FACT there are many stall-spin accidents makes us want to talk about this area and attempt to get it down to simple stuff, because there really isn't that much to it.

We discussed alpha and stalling, and in summing up, said we stalled because we got too slow for the way we were flying, whether straight and level or in any way extra g's are put on the airplane—that's mostly during turns although a sharp pull-up can cause excess g's too.

An added complexity in stalling out of turns is misuse of the controls—mostly ailerons. This can flip the airplane into a spin either in the direction of the turn or in the opposite direction (called "entering over the top").

But control misuse is serious only when one is too slow for the flight situation—high alpha and close to stall. (One can misuse controls at excessive high speed also, but that's another topic.)

How to stop all this nonsense? Get the nose down! Reduce alpha! Clean the wing of separated air!

For a bit we have to talk about things you don't see. In this case it's that flow separation when alpha gets too high. We've seen the classic drawing of air burbling as alpha gets high enough to be approaching stall (page 34). The point of the drawing, and the key, is that the disturbed air—separated flow—increases drag and kills lift.

$C_{L, max}$

Alpha, in numbers, is small: Fly the airplane at its maximum lift and alpha is, say 16°. The flow isn't separated, the wing is lifting with all it's got. In the trade that's called the alpha of $C_{L, max}$ —maximum lift coefficient. But increase just a little bit more and the flow begins to separate—we're leaving maximum lift territory and quickly approaching stall country! Only a 2° increase in alpha beyond $C_{L, max}$ on some wing sections will result in a 44 percent loss of lift! Some sections are better, some worse, but they all are of impressive magnitude.

Now—big point—reduce alpha that few degrees and the flow smooths out—reattaches; lift comes back, drag reduces, and we're back in business.

How do we reduce alpha? Just move the stick, or wheel, forward; sometimes simply releasing the back pressure is enough.

If we're well stalled we may have to push ahead more, but really it isn't much.

It Shakes

Just to be certain we understand: The flow isn't all smooth at one alpha and then, just a degree more, all gone to pieces. No, it progresses, and separation begins in little amounts, generally starting near the trailing edge of the wing root. Mostly we feel the separated flow—the chopped-up air—crossing the tail area and making it shake. It starts as a subtle nibble in the feel of the controls, but the more it separates the more the tail shakes. I've been in a well-developed stall in a 747, and you cannot imagine how much that big airplane shakes—kinda scary, but it holds together and recovers nicely.

This shaking that starts as a nibble and ends as a dog-shaking experience is good warning that one is getting into a stall area and it's time to release back pressure or push ahead a little.

Unfortunately the amount of shaking that warns one is different for different airplanes—some have very little warning of this nature and stall comes as a big surprise. Often these are airplanes with the horizontal stabilizer up high—T tails—and some are bad enough that stall-warning devices are required *plus* a stick pusher that automatically pushes ahead on the elevator control when alpha gets too high. But other tail configurations can be sneaky with little warning also. My Monocoupe—circa 1930—with its low-stabilizer elevator design, would pay off without the courtesy of even a little quiver. It didn't have a stall warning either, so one had to be alert.

It Takes More Than Stall Warning

Most airplanes today have stall-warning devices—bells, whistles or horns that say you're getting close to stall. But even with them people stall when they shouldn't. I like an airplane that naturally shakes and quivers when it gets close to stall. In exploring a new airplane's characteristics one of the first things I like to do is stall it and feel what sort of warning it gives.

When flying gliders I turn a lot and bank steeply in thermals to try and stay in the core of maximum lift and go up. I'm in steep turns just a few knots above stall. I want to be in a maximum lift situation—near $C_{L, max}$—so I'll climb the best possible, but we never want to get so slow that any separation begins, because the increased drag and loss of lift ruins the whole thing.

My present sailplane circles well at forty-seven knots; slow it to forty-three knots and it doesn't climb for sour apples. When the speed gets down to forty-three knots you feel a little nibble in the smoothness of flight. It is flow beginning to separate. When that happens, just releasing back pressure a mite stops the nibble, and you know you're flying efficiently again. Sometimes you circle in thermals right close to stall for long periods.

So you can circle in that glider at forty-seven knots and visualize the classic drawing of a wing with smooth flow. You pull back to forty-three knots and feel the nibble, visualize the flow starting to separate as it does in the drawing—push ahead, the drawing with smooth flow; pull back, the drawing with separation; pull back and feel the nibble, let the stick go a tiny bit forward and feel the nibble stop. I've circled for long periods just playing with this, and it makes all the stall business very clear.

But a pilot should be able to recognize when stall is near without any horns, shaking or whatever if he's watching the numbers—indicated airspeed (IAS)—relating it to his flight situation and realizing what situation he's in. It's obvious that more attention to stall is required if we're circling tight and low than if we're cruising along straight and level. There are times and situations where one's attention should be very much on the speed-stall relationship. This awareness is helped by being a good scanner, one who doesn't allow attention to become riveted on only one thing.

A typical goof-off would go like this: turning into final from base leg, pilot observes pattern is too wide so makes a steep turn to get around and line up for final; is so interested in seeing how the turn is getting the airplane lined up doesn't notice it has lost airspeed and is going too slowly for the bank being used—especially likely if the approach is low and the glide subconsciously being stretched; bingo, a spin.

The Nose!

Now let's see what we do if we get too close to stall and flow separation has started. It's simple, GET THE NOSE DOWN!

And here I have arguments with some of the stall methods being taught today. There's too much emphasis on recovery from *approach* to stall rather than a full stall. To make it worse, much instructing and checking in this area emphasizes the use of power more than it does getting the nose down for recovery.

What we really need is a regime that starts with approach to stall, but goes on to full stall.

Instructor: "See, feel that nibble? Now keep on slowing down—the nibble getting more pronounced? Keep on slowing—notice the shaking? Keep holding back—don't let up!" And one goes right on into stall until the airplane pays off, enters a spin or sits there with the nose bobbing up and down and everything shaking wildly.

In this shaky, confused state it's simple to demonstrate how pushing the nose down stops the shaking and gets things back to normal, albeit we're gaining speed and losing altitude.

Not Power Alone

This is where the power business comes in—to teach recovery with minimum altitude loss. But this can be a nervous way of doing business because the cart can get ahead of the horse. The horse being alpha. If the flow has separated and stall developed, alpha *has* to be reduced first! No amount of available power will "pull" one out of stall as long as the wing is stalled and the flow separated. So we're back to number one, GET THE NOSE DOWN!

If we're in a steep turn, *down* may not be precisely it, but it's all the same and means to push ahead, rotate so the wing has less alpha and flow begins to reattach.

After alpha has been reduced to an unseparated condition we want to recover and fly level again. This is a delicate area as we allow speed to increase, begin to raise the nose and add power. Actually they are almost done simultaneously. The dangerous point, however, is that power might be applied and the nose raised *before the nose has been lowered enough to clean the wing of separated flow,* and that can be very bad because a strong possibility exists that entry into a deep stall will occur.

In a condition of stall near the ground with all the scary feeling and near panic that may occur, the nose may have hardly been pushed over at all, but the power slammed on with mucho gusto as one tries to avoid hitting the ground; however, the stall hasn't been cured, and in all likelihood a spin will develop and that's that!

If we stall, or start to, close to the ground, we have to face the fact that we may get even closer before the stall is cured, because it is necesssary to get the nose down—and it takes a good chunk of intestinal fortitude to push the nose toward the upward rushing earth. But brushing along the tree tops under control with a clean wing is lots better than spinning into them.

Once the wing is clean, alpha out of stall range, then we can pour on power and get the nose up as long as we have sufficient speed and don't yank it up! Remember, stall can occur at higher speed if there are g loads on the airplane. So if our pull-up, in our exuberance to miss the ground, is too sharp, we increase g's and could well stall again. So our intestinal fortitude is called upon once again to help us push the nose at the earth and then pull it up gently as we apply power.

Spins

The big point is that pilots should know the complete stall, spin entry and recovery. Despite the FAA and manufacturers, any pilot who hasn't been in and out of spins enough to handle them just isn't a complete pilot.

Before my son soloed we did spins in our Cessna 120—chutes on—from all sorts of positions: straight ahead, out of steep turns, crossed controls and the lot. I wouldn't have felt comfortable with him soloing unless he knew spins, their recognition and recovery. Really they are not terrifying, but rather fun.

So to sum up—stall occurs above a certain alpha.

Alpha and speed are not related frequently enough to be interchangeable: Stall can occur at different airspeeds depending on g loads. Normally we fly level at one g, but the two g's of a 60° banked turn translate into a 40 percent higher stall speed.

We don't "see" alpha except in a few airplanes equipped with alpha indication, so except for knowledge of the theory we might as well forget it and relate stall to indicated airspeed. However, we must be aware that stall IAS is different with different flight situations; straight and level has one speed, but a turn has another and so does a pull-up; stall speed also increases as we put more weight in the airplane.

We cannot know and memorize all these speeds, but we can suspect too slow a speed for our situation, and we can feel and be alert to the closeness of stall and recognize it as it begins, by shaking, control feel and warning devices.

We can keep out of situations where a surprise stall might do us in—low and tight as in circling a friend's house, for instance.

Clean the Wing

To correct a stall condition, forward movement of the control is required and comes first! Even in turns, nose forward, cleaning the wing comes before unbanking even though the actions may follow close enough to appear as one. Power then follows.

It's all very easy if we scan and are observant and remember that first we need a "clean" wing or the stall isn't cured.

A Different Story

There's a situation that has received a lot of attention: It's when airspeed falls and we're headed for stall and everything says, "Get the nose down!" but actually we have to get the nose up—and add power—lots of power.

This occurs almost exclusively in wind shear conditions—particularly with jet types. Jets, especially, are affected because applying jet power doesn't come out the same as applying power to a propeller airplane. The jet engine's power response—the time between when you open the throttle and thrust begins to do something for you—is slower than with a propeller airplane. Also, with a pure jet, one doesn't get the advantage of air flow from the propeller over the wing. This is an important difference between pure jet and propeller airplanes. The lift from the air a propeller drives across the wing, and the amount deflected downward by the flaps, can increase lift in the order of 30 percent without any alpha change—pulling back on the wheel. In a pure jet there's none of this except possibly a small amount if the engine thrust line is such that it gives an upward vector. So the only way to increase lift is by increasing alpha, and since this increases drag lots of power is required—it's necessary to get the throttles forward a good lusty amount as the nose is raised.

Now this is tricky business indeed and must be done with expertise. Where does this happen? Classically during approach to landing.

A sudden wind or air movement change that results in big airspeed loss makes the airplane appear to be headed for stall. But pushing the nose over at low altitude during landing approach will result in altitude loss when there isn't room to lose any. The key is that the airplane *isn't as yet stalled,* and the nose can be raised to get closer to the alpha of $C_{L. max}$ to try and stop it from falling out of the sky.

Power has to go with raising the nose, all the power available. Sometimes one can get awfully close to stall doing this—even up to where the stick shaker is beginning to shake. But, as we said previously, the stick shaker is set for an alpha *nearing* stall and not *at* stall, so there's a margin to work with, albeit a very slim and nervous one.

The airplane will fly out of the decaying airspeed condition quickly, or if it's severe enough, and it can be, hit the ground. But increasing alpha and pouring on thrust is what one has to do if caught in such a drastic position.

As we said, this is mostly a jet condition; a propeller airplane would recover much better with its snappy power response and instant lift as the prop shoves air over the wing. But don't get a false sense of security over this—it can happen to propeller airplanes too, especially single engine ones.

In no way should this be thought of as the thing to do when stalled at low level—we have to clean the wing of separated air flow in that case.

This situation we've just talked about is a very tricky one that, hopefully, only pros will face. But the way to cure it is not to get in the condition in the first place. We're going to talk about that next.

9

The Business of Shear

A MYSTERIOUS, sometimes awesome, aura about wind shear has developed. Research has attached words to it such as downburst, microburst, miniburst and others that are a fancy way to describe what's been going on ever since the first thunderstorm was fired up, the first wind slammed into a mountain range to tumble over it, and the first air mass became unstable.

Interesting, but sometimes confusing because pilots wonder what to do about it—how to know where it is—where it has been hiding all these years? Well, let's go back to basics and try to sort it out.

Nothing New

Shear is part of our everyday flying life—realistically there's never a day we fly that shear isn't experienced in some degree.

Simply, shear is where winds of different velocities meet each other. All turbulence, as my friend Captain Paul Soderlind, the supreme technical airman, points out, is the result of shear. A simple "bump" is a piece of rising air—we bump when we fly through the edge of it, the boundary between where we were flying and where we enter the shaft of rising air, air of different velocity. A gust is where the wind velocity changes; the rotor of a mountain wave is a confused bunch of tumbling air—air of different velocities. The so-called downbursts are shafts of descending air no different from a little bump except one big bunch bigger.

Almost every time we land, shear is part of the action. It's routine in our lives.

Generally we approach to land into the wind. The wind velocity aloft is more than it is close to the ground, so the velocity decreases during our descent toward the runway. We lose airspeed as we go through this changing wind velocity, but most times it's of a gentle nature, and we hardly notice our juggling of stick or throttle.

But on those gusty days, with more dramatic velocity changes—and think of how many times this has happened to you—we have big sink approaching the end of the runway. We pour on the coal—or in a glider slam the spoilers shut—to get some energy back into our aircraft and overcome the airspeed loss. Big deal? Not really, just routine.

A Matter of Amount

So what's the difference between that and a downburst or whatever burst you want to call it? Amount; there's a big airspeed loss in a violent burst, plus a vertical vector that aggravates the situation. Vertical vector? Simply, it means that while the airspeed is changing in velocity, it also has a down direction that makes things worse. But forget that, because the result is the same—we lose airspeed and, so, lift.

If the numbers are within the capabilities of our power available as we increase alpha, we fly out of it—if not we're in deep trouble.

Answer—stay out of severe conditions no matter what they call them. How? It's not all that difficult or mysterious. Let's talk about it.

Since the "invention" of downbursts and all that goes with

them great effort has been made to warn pilots of these conditions as they approach an airport. Sounds fine, BUT—

Gadgets

First of all, the effort has the horse and wagon reversed. What we really need is something in the airplane to tell the pilot where these severe conditions are—immediately! Instead the effort has been to spot where the conditions are by ground observation— signals from wind-measuring devices on different locations around an airport are computerized and then sent to the pilot. (There's research being done using Doppler radar, on the ground, to tell where these things are, and that promises to be an improvement—but it still comes from the ground.)

To a layman this sounds great, but the layman doesn't realize that the time delay in transmitting the information just about nullifies its usefulness. These bursts of wind change happen far faster than the time it takes to find them and then send a radio message to the pilot. There's also the confusion of the pilot being able, with the data sent him, to determine *exactly* where it's located. It doesn't tell the pilot how to cope with it either. Instrumentation for that is needed—better alpha information, ground speed versus airspeed or energy data, presented in a usable form to alert the pilot to a high rate of airspeed and/or aircraft energy change.

All the ground-based data does is say there's trouble in the area and you'd better watch out! While I don't knock a try at sending information, pilots must realize it doesn't solve problems, and they cannot depend solely on the shear information. In other words we shouldn't relax into a feeling that everything is okay because there hasn't been a wind shear warning broadcast. There are always problems with sending information from the ground.

Any time an extra person is added in the chain and a requirement for communicating introduced, one has automatically put in a factor that will fail from time to time; the communications are misunderstood or sent incorrectly; the communicating doesn't get done (this has happened during shift changes—a good example is when one tower shift was sending information that braking action was poor, but the next shift didn't catch it, so didn't send it, and an airplane went off the end of the runway—at Boston, a DC-10), or it's put on the Automatic Terminal Information Service (ATIS), which often is old data, shot out at tobacco auctioneer's rate of talk so it's difficult to understand; is missed because we're too busy with ATC (Air Traffic Control) and flying the airplane to try and listen to it more than once when it's poorly done or has such a mass of information we cannot get it all in one listen—too much information.

Voice communication, which is big in flying, is a poor way of doing business, and it's a burden that has caused many accidents and incidents. The less talk the better even though the trend seems to be for more.

You Suffer

But the solutions are typically the kind pilots have suffered from all their lives—solutions made by bureaucrats and people who aren't pilots and haven't seen the action—or who are minimally qualified or not current. This is a *serious fault* in flying, one not confined to wind-shear solutions, and any pilot should be aware that many things presented are not only of little use, but may dupe us into wrong decisions. Pilots are on their own and should use information only as it fills in blank spaces in the data which they need to make judgments. There's a big difference between factual information and information that has a decision injected into it by someone other than the pilot; this is hazardous stuff. WE SHOULD MAKE OUR OWN DECISIONS. This is a little far

afield from wind shear, but it's very important. Now to get back
on course.

We Are on Our Own

There is value in the shear warning as long as we know its limitations, but it isn't going to be available everywhere; the costs
will prohibit the installation except on key airline airports. There
are about 6,000 public airports in the USA; FAA's budget has 110
scheduled for shear monitoring systems through 1985—so what
happens to pilots flying into the other 5,890 airports?

Well, it gets around to the point we've been harping on; pilots
are on their own and have to look for themselves! It's never been
any different.

A lot of pilots had flown a lot of years before the downburst,
microburst et al. were "invented." There probably were accidents because of it, but all in all the record was probably as good
as now. Why? And this is a *key* point. Pilots knew that squirrelly
winds and violent things go on near thunderstorms. Answer, stay
away from landing and taking off when thunderstorms are close to
an airport! Simple. Pilots knew it back when—airline companies
did too. Joe Browne of TWA published an interesting bulletin
about wind shear and its hazards for TWA's pilots in the 1950s.

Jet aircraft may have increased the problem because of their
different response, but we'd flown a lot of jet hours too before this
"new" knowledge came on the scene.

The Record

A compilation of twenty-eight shear incidents and accidents
over an 18-year period shows that twenty-five of them were during thunderstorm conditions. One of the others was in a strong
mountain lee wave during a snowstorm; another, an incident with

no injuries, was during conditions of fog and drizzle at La Guardia when the wind changed from a 42-knot tail wind at 1500 feet to a 5-knot head wind on the ground. This isn't an unusual condition in New York, with a low off Long Island. Another was during a frontal condition landing in rain and fog. The rest, as we said, were with thunderstorms or heavy rain showers close to the airport.

If there are thunderstorms around the airport, what's too close for taking off or landing? I don't know. Neither does anyone else. There are too many variables related to what kind of a thunderstorm—big, small, air mass, prefrontal, frontal. It comes down to judgment.

The Big Picture

One key is to know what the general weather setup is that will tell us what kind of thunderstorm it is. We also must obtain an up-to-date reading of weather reports at the airport we're headed for or leaving *and airports in the general area for a couple of hundred miles;* surface winds, temperature changes, amount of precipitation and pressure changes all tell a story about what to expect.

Northwest Orient Airlines has a perfect record of no shear problems—no passenger injuries in turbulence either—and much of it can be attributed to their chief meteorologist, Dan Sowa, and his staff and their ability to forecast the conditions and get the word out to the pilots. This proves that weather observation and forecasts can go a long way toward helping pilots avoid the conditions. The bottom line, of course, is: When in doubt, don't! Especially, don't race a thunderstorm to an airport! And don't rush to take off before an approaching storm hits! Big important items.

This isn't a weather book—we did one on that subject (*Weather Flying*—Macmillan), but certain points of weather can be resaid a thousand times to benefit. And a key one is to know what's going on—not just a narrow, horse-blinder piece of information about the airport we're interested in, but about a wide area around it plus the big picture setup.

Shear isn't found only in thunderstorms. A strong overrunning of air as part of a warm front: Kansas City, Missouri, summer night, warm, still, no wind. We're coming from the north; ground speed's been slow, but with no wind on the surface we can land straight in. As we descend we're suddenly falling out of the sky. Why? There's one heck of a wind aloft even down low, close to the ground. It's from the southwest at nearly 50 knots. The slow ground speed should have tipped us off, or we'd have known it if we had inspected the winds aloft carefully. Near the ground there was hardly any wind—that's shear and why we had trouble.

Downwind of mountains the air spills, even reverses, especially if there are waves and the airport is close to or in the rotor.

Valleys

At valley airports, the wind is often close to a runway's direction. We take off without thinking about the wind aloft—or land and find impressive shear. What happened? Valleys make winds phlegmatic, light and variable, or straighten them out to kind of favor one runway. Our tendency is to use the most convenient runway. Wrong. What we should be using is the runway that will put us into the prevailing flow—the wind of the general flow caused by the high or low over us.

Here in Sugarbush, Vermont, the convenient runway is 22, but the wind aloft may be whistling from the north; tow plane and glider take off the convenient way, southwest, because the wind is almost calm on the ground. You can watch with fascination; the combination gets off well and starts to climb briskly—then, as they enter the upper wind flow, there's a sagging of them both, a

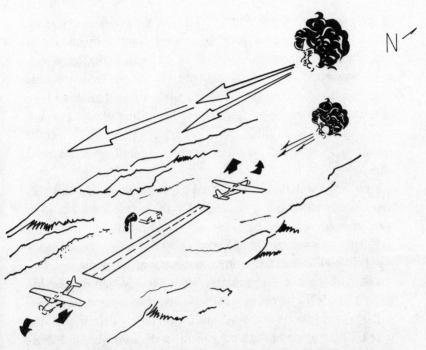

Light wind on the ground, strong from the north aloft. The airplane taking off north is going into an increasing head wind; its nose tends to pitch up and it climbs better with increasing altitude. But the airplane taking off south is going into an increasing tail wind; its nose tends to drop and climb deteriorates with altitude. The airplane taking off north is doing it right.

struggle until enough speed is made up to overcome the airspeed loss; it can make one nervous. Fortunately we see less of this as time goes on, because experience has sharpened us all and we look at the wind aloft, the general flow, before setting up takeoff.

What's the Direction?

A major key to all this is how conscious we are of the general wind. Sometimes we act as though all flying were done on the ground, because we seem to be predominately interested in ground weather reports. But a real part of the action is above us, especially what the wind is doing as soon as we're up and out of the influence of the ground: hills, valleys, mountains, large bodies of water and so on. A pilot should ask for and know what the wind is at the first level it's reported; also, know if there's a high or low dominating the area, which is a strong hint of what the general wind flow is. Without any information a pilot can look at the clouds and see which way they are moving and sense the wind aloft.

Knowing these things we can take off toward a wind that will increasingly be on our nose; and we'll be aware of what kind of wind change there will be as we descend to land.

Keeping away from thunderstorms when taking off and landing, being aware that winds in mountainous areas can be very different aloft from on the ground, realizing that instability near the ground or aloft can cause wind velocity changes and direction, will all provide hefty armor against the problem of shear. It's also wise to think again of the strong fact that the discovery and analysis of conditions, and decision on how to cope with them, is up to the pilot; the stuff they send from the ground, while useful, doesn't solve the problem.

10

Some Important Points

BEFORE WE BEGIN to walk around the airplane and inspect it for flight we really should have answered the question, "What are we going to do on this flight?"

Whether it's to be a hop around the field or a long cross-country we ought to have a plan before we fling ourselves into the sky.

Not long ago I went on a test hop at the Boeing factory in a 757. We were to do engine cuts and then evaluate restarting them from a windmilling condition at certain airspeeds. This is pretty routine and boils down to stabilizing at an airspeed, cutting an engine and then after it's stabilized, start it again taking certain data. (It's a great airplane with an engine out.)

The objective was to do this a number of times with different conditions—as I recall we cut engines about 15 times. The test pilots and crew didn't just take off and then decide what to do. No, it was written out in a four-page document that everyone involved studied and talked over before takeoff. When we got in the air our ATC clearance had been approved, and we climbed on course to altitude, the airplane was set up to the parameters the test document called for, and the tests began: no fooling around, no indecision, no wasted time. A neat operation.

A Plan

Of course that's the extreme. But let's say we're going to get our 172 out and shoot some landings to tune our skills and exercise the airplane. Have we thought out before takeoff what kind of landings we're going to do—power off, power on? Full flap, partial flap, no flap? Full stop, touch and go? Which ones first? Are we going to take off and circle in the pattern for an immediate landing, or go out to the practice area for a limbering up first? If we go out to the practice area what are we going to do? Steep turns? Stalls? Didos?

Did we think, before we even got aboard, what the wind was, which runway is being used, how heavy the traffic is, which way we'll turn to get out to the practice area?

Of course we're not going to make a four-page document of the plan as they did at Boeing, and we'll leave ourselves the fun of flexibility, but we think about it enough before we fly to remove uncertainty. We don't want to find ourselves trying to decide what to do first and which way to go when we should be using our concentration on flying the airplane during the busy time during and right after takeoff.

The more extensive the flight—cross-country with weather —the more we ought to have well in mind what our plan of attack is and what we're going to do. It creates a relaxed feeling and reduces the extraneous thoughts that make the immediate task more difficult.

A key to all flying is to do things, or plan them, during times when we are free from other tasks. It's a constant clever game of doing things during periods that are free so we're as little hampered as possible when the heat's on and we're busy. It's as simple as digging out the car keys inside where it's warm and lighted rather than fumbling around for them outside in the cold and dark.

Fly Out Front

All this relates to keeping ahead of the airplane, which is one of the solid-gold principles of flying. The good pilots are way ahead of their airplane. What does it mean? Just what we've been talking about: knowing in advance what we're going to do; setting things up before the action to relieve the work load during busy moments.

It's also knowing weather in advance and what it might or might not do, so we aren't suddenly faced with surprises and an almost desperate need to get more weather information and digest it during a packed-full flying period that has ATC problems, ice or thunderstorms and the lot.

It's planning an arrival, computing when we should start our descent to arrive near the airport at a useful altitude for the landing pattern. It's getting the airplane slowed down so there's ample time to lower flaps and landing gear. It's setting the airplane up for landing at the outer marker so that there isn't anything to change or fret about during the high concentration of an instrument approach except the approach—all that's left to do is chop the throttles and land when we're sure the runway is "in the bag."

We don't fly with an intense concentration all the time. There are long periods empty of any immediate tasks—it's almost boring and has spawned the famous statement that flying is "hours of boredom interrupted by moments of stark terror."

That may be an exaggeration, but it does contain some truth, especially if the pilot hasn't used those hours of "boredom" planning ahead, keeping in touch with weather, double-checking navigation and monitoring the airplane and its systems.

PHC

The moments of stark terror could better be called Periods of High Concentration (PHC). Coming down an ILS (Instrument Landing System) is a PHC, so is takeoff and landing—the list is long. But PHCs can be less hectic if we plan ahead and use the easy time to keep things neat and tight with an awareness of what's ahead and how we're going to cope with it. Doing this keeps the PHC from becoming a "moment of stark terror."

What

All kinds of things are possible to do in advance, some quite simple such as having all charts out and ready for an instrument approach—and studying the approach; some more complex such as getting the latest weather and having an alternate in mind plus your fuel situation computed to know how much will be available on arrival, how much it'll be necessary to have for flight to the alternate—so we'll know how long we can hold for ATC or if we can make a second approach, if necessary, before we have to depart for the alternate. It's one whale of a lot better to have this established and in mind before arrival rather than trying to figure it out while receiving a complicated ATC clearance and flying precise maneuvers.

The airplane ought to be set up ahead—heat needed *on,* checklists read and complied with as much as possible. (Checklists are used by all, or should be whether flying the simplest airplane or the most complex. They should be as short as safely possible and then read at a time that's least busy. That's all the attention we're going to give to them—there's no point in carrying on about checklists; they are nearly as much a part of flying today as the wings.)

In the back of one's mind is the runway's length and it's braking condition, what turbulence we may have, the wind and what sort of drift there will be on approach and break out—the list goes on, but the objective is obvious; review anything that could be done in advance and then do it. A good pilot is always thinking in these terms, being ahead not only in the sense of what we've been talking about, but also in the deeper sense of what can be done to cope with the flight if things don't go as expected. The weather turns sour, there's an unexpected, long ATC delay, an engine failure—the thinking never stops.

Not Nervous

But we don't want to give the impression that good pilots go around in a constant state of nervous apprehension—they don't. Because they do think about possibilities and how they can be ahead of and understand them, their flying is more relaxed, they have things in hand and under control. It isn't knowing that makes us jumpy, rather it's the unknown. Good pilots keep that to a minimum.

11

Before We Start

THERE'S NOT MUCH to talk about in preflighting an airplane. We've had that drilled into us, and it's a question of personality. Some people are conscientious and others are sloppy. One does a thorough job and the other takes a look and is satisfied if he sees nothin' hangin' or drippin'.

Of course the hangin' and drippin' people may well come a cropper. That's their problem, but it does bring out a point about air safety—you cannot change the traits of some people, and they will have more accidents than others. The solution to the problem isn't in the ken of this book; perhaps it could be found—at least explored—on a psychologist's couch.

Before we got off on that we were talking about preflight, and said that enough had been talked about and could be found in manuals so that we wouldn't dwell on it. But you cannot flip by it without a couple of observations.

Distractions

Preflight is serious business, and when we go through the ritual it should have our undivided attention. This we probably give it, but outside forces often break in: A friend follows us around the airplane dramatizing about an almost fatal bout with weather, or his or her latest girl/boy friend or any talk that's not centered on the preflight. You stop what you're doing to be polite or respond to the blathering, then resume the preflight with an excellent chance that you've passed by an item.

We get this a lot assembling gliders—it's a great time for other glider pilots to drift by and carry on about their latest soaring adventures or theories, thoughtlessly distracting you. Missing things while assembling a glider can be very serious, as, for example, not connecting the elevator and then being towed into the air to discover there isn't any elevator control! Imagination? No, it has really happened—more than once. Serious omissions have occurred on airplane preflights too.

Distractions are bad news, and personally I've become hard-nosed about them. If one is interrupted while preflighting an airplane or assembling a glider or, for that matter, checking weather, making out a flight plan or other important functions that require concentration, distractors should be politely told to hold off—you'll answer or listen later. It's no time to be bashful!

We can be the distraction ourselves if we break in the middle of a preflight or whatever task we're doing and then come back later to pick up where we left off—we may pick up two items past where we stopped, missing them. If it's necessary to interrupt, then when we resume, we ought to start over from the beginning.

Fuel

Aside from the nuts and bolts part of a preflight there's the matter of fuel. Is it in the tanks, is there enough, are the tanks secure? Obvious stuff, but one of the major causes of power loss—engines stopping—is running out of fuel, and this goes from little singles to big transports. Running out of fuel means a pilot screwed up. You can rationalize all kinds of things, but you're only ducking the real issue. The pilot screwed up!

We have all kinds of safeguards in airplanes, and big airline types are full of redundancy—multiple generators, pressurization

systems, instruments, even pilots—there is more than one of each
so if one fails there's another to get home on. Not so with fuel.
There's one load of fuel, and when it's gone all comes to a stop!
It's pretty obvious, then, that having enough fuel and using it
wisely is a high priority item on the pilot's list and one he or she
should have intimate awareness of.

Fuel can cause a problem because there wasn't enough put on
board and the pilot didn't check to see that there was. In flight,
head winds slow us down and fuel runs short; proper, up-to-the
minute navigation keeps the pilot aware of this situation, and he
does something about it before it becomes critical.

Pilots believe in fuel gauges more than they should. Big airplane fuel gauges are pretty good, but they have problems from
time to time, and there is a built-in error that can run from one to
six percent. If one is flirting with empty tanks, that can be serious—an airliner made a tragic forced landing because of this. Little airplanes, singles and such, have fuel gauges that are pathetic:
bouncing corks and the like. Even though the gauge has an impressive needle reading the amount, the needle is simply connected to and getting the word from a cork! You only really know
when it's either full or empty, because in those positions the cork
stops bouncing; in between, as it bobbles about, the amount can
be anything.

No Gauges

We should keep track of fuel usage as though the airplane had
NO gauges! This isn't an automobile—we don't pull over to the
side of the road and say, "Ah, shucks," if we run out. In flight
there's a much bigger problem than that—there are no filling stations in the sky! (Someone is bound to pick up on that and start
talking about refueling in flight—that's military, and I'm sure a
four-engine jet tanker wouldn't slide in front of my 172 and pass
a hose to me—or to a 747 either.)

How to keep tabs? First, know how much is in the tanks at take-off, and not by glancing at the gauges! We look in the tanks or stick them, or, on airlines, make certain of the paper work—fuel remaining when the airplane arrived plus the amount added, the total then checked against the gauges. If in doubt we should have enough guts to request that the tanks be dipsticked.

A Grease Pencil

In other airplanes a valuable aid in the cockpit is a red grease pencil. When my 172 is filled the tank hours are marked with a red grease pencil, on a corner of the windshield where it will not obstruct vision. When the airplane is flown next the tach hours can be noted and compared with those when filled. Then you know how many hours have been used out of the tanks. Knowing quite precisely how many gallons per hour the 172 burns, you have an idea of what's remaining. The filler caps should be checked along with a look in the tanks, and all this checked against the gauges, taking into account that they aren't accurate. The grease-pencil marking is also helpful when another person flies the airplane and wants an idea of the fuel situation and you're not around to tell them—my son and I find it so with the 172. (The grease pencil is useful during instrument approaches also. You can make a mark on the altimeter at the minimum altitude you want to descend to as a reminder—new fancy altimeters have "bugs" that can be set for this, but a grease-pencil marking will do the job about as well.)

Keeping Tabs

Knowing how much we had at takeoff the job, in flight, is to keep track of the burn as we go along. (Airlines call fuel use "fuel burn.")

How much fuel used subtracted from what we had at takeoff gives us what's remaining. Then we know how far we can go under present conditions and whether we'll have enough reserves at destination to be comfortable, considering the weather conditions.

A Pencil and Paper

Keeping track is done with notes on paper, not simply in one's head, as easy as that may seem. In the heat of problems created by ATC, weather and all that, we can easily make mistakes or remember figures that actually were transposed or incorrect. Being able to refer to notes can make the important difference. (On any cross-country flight, or flight of longish duration, one should have a note pad to mark down time off and fuel at takeoff and other handy information.)

Reserves

The reserve is important, and one way of getting in trouble is by cutting reserves too close. I have long-range tanks in my 172. I get stiff and bored, hungry and thirsty when the tanks get down to about half full. I begin to look for a place to land. Big reserve—very comfortable flying.

Flying airliners I'd cut reserves closer than I ever do in a single. Why? Control is better. Airline pilots are better informed on current weather, are more up-to-date with it because there's help from company dispatch. The airplane and system have the best in weather flying capability. The fuel-flow readings are more accurate, and how much we've used can be precisely determined. Strong head winds affect a jet less because its true airspeed is so high that an unexpected fifty-knot head wind over a 200-mile distance, for example, is only going to mean three more minutes—

in a 172 it would add one hour and thirty-one minutes! If that 200 miles has a bunch of bad weather with no place in it to land, you really need enough fuel to go the full distance—in a jet it's no sweat; in a 172 it may be an unwanted adventure! That's an extreme, but it can be scaled to other aircraft with other true airspeeds, and there's still an impressive difference.

Flying an airliner the copilot relieves the pilot of much of the work, and on many aircraft, a second officer is a further aid, especially in keeping an accurate fuel inventory. Also supporting you is the organization on the ground—it's a team effort.

But out there on your own it's a different ball game. You fly it yourself, juggle ATC problems, scrounge for weather, keep tabs on fuel and reserves, are hampered by the slower ground speed and bigger drift angles; it's a tougher task than the airline pilot has—and all those things are reasons why I want more fuel reserves flying a Cessna 172 than a Boeing 747.

Fuel, then, is really a very important part of preflight—not just that it's on board, but the mulling over the winds and weather we're about to launch into.

Water

An added note on fuel is the matter of draining and checking for water. This is important and *never* should be passed over when fuel is added or the airplane has been sitting any length of time. Periodically we hear of engines quitting because of water in the fuel. The probability of having water has been reduced from the days of flying a Monocoupe when every drop that went in the airplane was put through a chamois to check for water and dirt. But the problem hasn't been reduced 100 percent and still is serious and probably will be in the future.

In this day and age we also want to be certain it's the kind of fuel we want—not just the color and octane, but if gasoline or kerosene—jet fuel; they have been swapped accidentally and internal combustion engines don't run on jet fuel.

Fuel System

As long as we're talking about fuel we ought to touch on the importance of knowing the fuel system *very* well. A big portion of engine failures—multi or single—are the result of a fuel-system foul-up—not simply running out of fuel (although that happens), but other causes such as running out on one tank and landing dead stick with fuel remaining in another tank! Or using the system improperly so fuel will not drain from all tanks. Examples of various mix-ups in fuel-system use could take up quite a few lines of type.

The simple cure is to know the fuel system very, very well. It should be studied so there are no doubts on its sequence of use, what turns what on, what pumps are required and the amount of usable fuel available (not what the tanks hold, but how much of what they hold can be used—the remainder slopping around in a corner, but never going down the pipe to the engine, is useless).

If one has an intimate knowledge of the fuel system the chances of an engine quitting because of mismanagement are reduced to almost zero. The other benefit should a failure occur is that checking the fuel system to see if fuel starvation is the problem can be done quickly and confidently because we know what we're looking at.

An engine cannot live without fuel, so having enough and knowing how it gets to the engine is a big first basic in flying.

It Has To Be Clean

Before takeoff we should have a flawless airplane; to be certain it's flawless is part of preflight. An obvious item that keeps being overlooked or disregarded is the matter of taking off with frost or ice on wings—an airplane covered with such is by no means flaw-less!

This goes for little airplanes as well as big ones, and an area exists that really hasn't been made clear enough to assure us that the trouble will not repeat itself tonight.

First, we all agree that it's very bad to take off with anything on the wings that shouldn't be there. Mostly we're talking about frozen things. We could go into lengthy aerodynamic reasons, but none would do much better than to say that frozen particles on the wing distort the airflow and, in a closely related way, separate it as in or near a stall. Sometimes it's pretty impressive. The more modern the wing—slick laminar flow type—the more sensitive it is. A coating of frozen precipitation sticking on the wing tip of a modern airline-type aircraft ONLY as rough as No. 200 sand-paper—about like the coating of sand on the bottom of a bird cage—can raise the stall speed 30 percent! It does other things too: The tips stall and quit lifting, but the root near the fuselage doesn't. The wing is swept, so there's lift forward, near the root,

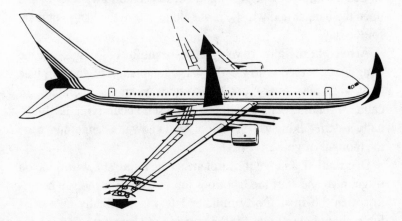

Tip stall and pitch up of swept wing aircraft. Root has clean flow and is lifting, tip has disturbed flow and is settling. Tip is back, root forward so aircraft is "twisted" to pitch nose up.

but none back at the tips, so the airplane pitches up. The pitch-up gets the root of the wing to a higher alpha and into the stall regime too. Then we've lost it all.

Old Wings Too

But wing sensitivity isn't restricted to new technology wings. I know, intimately, of a Bonanza trying a takeoff with frost on the wings that ended up in a ball of fire near the end of the runway— ditto in a different location with a D-18 Beech, which is an old design of high-lift wing section.

So any way we look at it, and being repetitious because it's worth repeating, trying to take off with frost, ice, snow and such on the wing is a very perilous thing to do.

And Small Aircraft

Little airplanes like my Cessna 172: I had to go to Boston early so tied the airplane out overnight, because I didn't want to try and open the hangar and wrestle it out alone before the gang got there for the day.

Arrived at the airport very early, beautiful fall dawn, but the wing was covered with frost! What a temptation to go. Airplane light—just me—over 5,000 feet of runway, cool temperature, air calm. A genuine confrontation with myself about trying it. But finally a stern talking to, ''You fool, you know it's dangerous, drop the thought of going.''

Disgruntled, I move the airplane so the rising sun will shine on it, get rags and start the laborious job of wiping as the sun begins to soften the frost. Forty minutes late when I finally take off I fume about being tardy for the meeting at Hanscome Field. I get there and make my excuses; it didn't matter, they understood. A few minutes later it was all forgotten.

The pressure to go is understandable, but the silliness of it, the realization of how unimportant being a little late really is, makes one feel good about the decision.

Two Parts

Now, bigger airplanes working in the environment of a busy airport, going to taxi out and depart in bad weather:
There are two parts to it—

1. Deicing
2. Anti-icing

Deicing means to clean the airplane of whatever has accumulated on it from being parked for less than half an hour to all night in conditions that can coat the wing: frost, ice, wet snow, freezing rain, freezing drizzle or combinations of them all.

Snow Can Fool Us

Sometimes dry snow that appears not to have stuck on the surfaces can fool you. You puff your breath on it and it blows away; you think it will blow off during takeoff, but it probably will not—air flow over the wing doesn't do it because of boundary-layer reasons too wordy to get into. Also, if the temperature hasn't been very cold there will likely be some firm stuff under the snow, maybe tiny granules clinging to the wing surface.

Whatever, we have to clean the wing—deice it. Most places are set up to do it with a hot mixture of glycol and water. Hot water alone will do it. But either way the wing must have all the ''junk'' removed, and then we're ready to fly. (It is important, as well, to remove all ice from the wing root area where it meets the fuselage; ice here can disturb flow that seriously affects control capability—ditto back at the tail stabilizer-fin juncture.)

That's Not All

Are we ready to go? No, because now we are interested in the second point, anti-icing. If there is any precipitation falling that will stick to the wing before we can take off we need anti-icing protection.

This is a very important area. There must be anti-icing fluid on the wing to protect it from gathering a frozen coating as we taxi or wait in line for takeoff.

If we deiced—cleaned the wing—with a mixture of glycol and water—we have some protection (we don't have any, of course, if we deiced only with hot water). But now we're in very danger-ous territory, because there is a misconception that a glycol-water solution on the wing will give sufficient protection. Not so, be-cause a glycol-water mixture, even if it's sprayed on the wing after it's been deiced, has a limited time of effectiveness—*a shorter time than most people think!* How long it's good for de-pends on conditions and mixtures. The worst condition is freezing rain, and in that, from tests done in Europe by the Scandinavians, a glycol-water mixture only gives protection for about three min-utes! If it's light wet snow, glycol and water will be good for a short fifteen minutes—twenty at the most!

This difference depends on conditions and the mixture of gly-col-water. Sometimes it's 50/50, on up to 100 percent glycol. This is a vague area too and depends on who's doing the operation and what manual they are reading. Also, going to 100 percent glycol is not a panacea because some water is needed for best ef-fectiveness. It's a tricky business that isn't always well adminis-tered in the U.S.A. But regardless of the mixture the protection is limited.

Delays on the runway are often long. Pilots squirm in their seats, squeezed in a situation between icing up and waiting to be number one for takeoff. It takes a lot of fortitude to give up and taxi back for more deicing when we've been waiting twenty minutes or more and know we'll be number one in another ten minutes. But this is what good pilots are made of; the stuff to make tough unpopular decisions.

A lot of research has been done in Europe on this problem, by the Scandinavians and Soviets particularly. They have come up with better ideas.

Results—the Europeans are very nervous with glycol-water mixtures, and while they use them (they cost less), they do not if there will be a long time between deicing and takeoff. If the time looks as though it will be long they use newer, "thicker" fluids that have a much longer "holding" time—such as forty-five minutes against glycol's fifteen. They have brand names: Killfrost, ABC/Hoechst and in the U.S.S.R., Artika-200; there are others, but they are all similar.

Typical operation: Paris, Charles De Gaulle Airport (CDG). A big airplane-type "car wash" on a taxiway. If you will be taking off soon—number one—you taxi through this. It squirts a hot, 85°C, mixture of glycol and water over the airplane to clean and anti-ice. After that, without delay because they know the glycol-water holding time is limited, you taxi to the runway and take off. *If*, however, there's going to be a delay between start-up and take-off, the spraying is done at the gate with the newer, thicker fluid.

The U.S.A. is studying the fluids—Europe has been using them for about five years.

The book of regulations is full of warnings to the pilot. FAA's Advisory Circular on the subject, No. 20-117, says, "Just prior to taking the active runway for takeoff or just prior to initiating takeoff roll, a visual pre-takeoff inspection should be made."

The FAA recognizes how impractical this is, and they go on to say so for a number of paragraphs with suggested procedures that must have made the person who wrote them feel specious. Example: You're number one at O'Hare with twenty airplanes behind you, and the tower says immediate takeoff! How do you make a visual inspection "prior to initiating takeoff roll"?

The final sentence in this section sums up, saying, "The decision to take off, following pre-takeoff inspection, remains the responsibility of the pilot in command."

So here we are again, it's the pilots' responsibility, and their ball game; pilots will still taxi out, get in line and wait for takeoff, stewing about how much good the glycol-water mixture is doing, worrying if it's beginning to stick out there. It's dark; you cannot see the wing surface. You open a window and reach out with your bare hand and feel the fuselage, you send the first or second officer back in the cabin to shine a light through a window over the wing and see how it looks—it looks confusing because the light bounces back, doesn't give a clear picture. You fret.

It doesn't relieve the fretting, but it's worth knowing that glycol-water mixtures are suspect; they are only good for a brief time. It also points up that strong decisions are necessary—taxiing back to have the airplane deiced and anti-iced again—nobody is there to help on this one. The only things around are the rules to put it firmly in your lap.

It's another of the lonesome-pilot decisions that flying has in abundance. One of the main purposes of this book is to point out that these responsibilities are placed on the pilot; it's part of the game so we'd best be prepared and not expect the deciding help from outside the cockpit—it's all yours and you take the blame. People used to ask me about my "high" airline pilot pay. My response was always the same, "I'm paid to take the blame."

The airplane is inspected; we know what we want to do on the flight; there's enough fuel aboard to feel comfortable with and the wings are clean. It's time to go.

Load

Well, not quite, because there's another area that demands being flawless before flight, and it has to do with weight and where it is.

The maximum gross weight of an airplane is a value established by the manufacturer and the FAA after considering strength and performance. There's no excuse for exceeding this gross weight unless we're on a ferry flight or some special mission and it has been cleared with the FAA and the manufacturer. Aside from that, it isn't worth the time and effort to wave our arms and expound on all the reasons gross weight shouldn't be exceeded—any pilot from student on knows the established valid reasons. If pilots insist on exceeding gross weight then we put them in the same category as pilots who try to take off with ice on their wings, dive and zoom houses, skip preflights and perform other senseless antics.

CG

At times, even religiously observing the max gross weight figure, we can get in trouble if the load isn't distributed correctly and the airplane is out of balance vis-à-vis the center of gravity (CG).

I flew an experimental airplane with a computer setup that could change the CG as well as the flight characteristics. Two sets of controls: one, the normal controls the safety pilot managed; the other, programmed to respond as a computer commanded. You could make the airplane, a Navion, fly like a 747 as far as control response and stability were concerned. Also, you could fly it as though the CG was out of limits.

We hear about all the bad things being out of CG limits can bring, but when you experience an out-of-limits rear CG that makes the airplane divergent you are impressed indeed—CG management takes on a clear meaning. What's divergent? Simply, when the nose goes up, for example, instead of it coming back down, as it normally does, to find the trimmed speed, it keeps right on going up—pushing forward on the elevator doesn't ruffle its feathers a bit—it keeps right on going up! You have a

very helpless feeling when the airplane doesn't answer the controls as it should—you're out of control!

A rearward CG is a nice thing to have—it relieves tail loads and
reduces drag—you perform better for the same amount of effort.
In gliders we get the CG as far aft as possible within the parameters of the design and good sense. But, as the CG gets too far back
the airplane becomes less stable—it's more of a handful to fly,
and if you're on instruments trying to make a delicate approach at
a specific speed, the speed is difficult to stay on. All this can occur even before the airplane has a CG so far back it's divergent.

The airplane-manual limits are designed to give a CG as far aft
as possible while still keeping the airplane stable. In other words
if we stay within the manual limits we'll not have a problem. But
go beyond the edge, even a tiny bit, and the airplane doesn't fly
as well; go farther out and it's worse, until finally it could be unmanageable. And with the CG out-of-limits aft, chances are it
would never recover from a spin should we get in one.

Too far forward can be just as ugly—try landing!

So those limits marked on that graph in the airplane manual are
for real. Unless we're completely stupid we stay well within
them.

12

Airplanes on the Ground

AIRPLANES HAVE to move and manuever on the ground, which isn't their natural element, and the landing gear, while important, is a bore to the designer and always a compromise. If it's retractable there's no place to put it and valuable space is used fitting it in; it's too narrow, too short, too stiff, not stiff enough; the wheels are too small; the brakes get too hot and wear out quickly; pants on the wheels make it difficult to put air in the tires; they collect mud, snow and slush, and you bang your shin on them getting in the airplane.

Airplanes have wing and control surfaces designed to face into the wind, but on the ground the wind may hit them from any angle and make the airplane difficult to manage.

The visibility isn't all that great, especially if you are flying an airplane with tail wheel or tail skid that causes visiblity over the nose to be almost nil. To see ahead while taxiing this kind it's necessary to go along like a wiggling snake. It's a pretty grim picture and perhaps a bit magnified, but while some airplanes are fairly good regarding landing gear and visibility, none are perfect and, really, why should they be—the airplane's designed to fly over the earth—not crawl along on it.

The important point is that the airplane, doing its thing, spends only a small portion of its total time on the ground where its progress is slow—it spends most time in the air where it can let out and

go. For these reasons we put up with its awkwardness while earth-
bound.

Easy Does It

A pilot, therefore, needs to realize these limitations and com-
promises and to live with them. It comes down to the simple point
that it is rather silly to hurry on the ground. A few extra minutes
spent bowing to the fact the airplane is not a good automobile and
needs tender care on the ground is well worthwhile. Airline pilots
trying to make schedule may scorn me on this—but they above all
should "hurry" only within the capabilities of aircraft and the airport's systems. A bent wing tip can mean a bent career in the simple example, or a catastrophe in the worst when fuel is spilled and
fires start.

Busy Busy

A busy airline airport can be a rather exciting place around terminals and taxiways. JFK about seven-thirty in the evening is a
mass of airplanes and ground equipment all moving and hurrying.
Some of the service vehicles are unbelievable, and I've had a
commissary truck play "chicken" with me when I was trying to
taxi a 747! I might have had a warped sense of admiration for his
crust, but I was furious at his audacity.

Working one's way through the maze of taxiways after getting
clearance from the tower—that came at you like the overpowering
rush of water from a fire hose in a string of lefts, rights, alphas,
poppas and other hunks of phonetic alphabet to tell you which
taxiways you must travel—is a delicate piece of business, especially when it's dark and raining or snowing. The miracle to me is
that we don't have a constant string of accidents in these areas;
that we don't is testimony, in great part, to the good judgment of
pilots.

A worrisome hazard is that through a mix-up of taxiways an airplane can get on the wrong one and wind up on an active runway, especially at night or in very reduced visibility. I've seen this happen and can remember one night at JFK when we were slowly moving up to takeoff position on Runway 22R and a mixed-up 747 pilot found himself on the takeoff runway headed into the traffic. It wasn't a dangerous situation because he could be seen, but it had humor, if you could keep your sense of it during the delay, while they sorted airplanes out and moved them around to let him get back where he belonged.

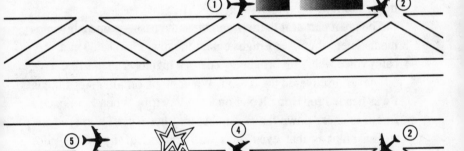

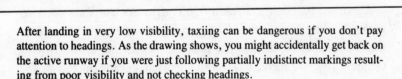

After landing in very low visibility, taxiing can be dangerous if you don't pay attention to headings. As the drawing shows, you might accidentally get back on the active runway if you were just following partially indistinct markings resulting from poor visibility and not checking headings.

Potential Disaster!

Condition: Very low visibility.

1. Aircraft lands (could be an abort).
2. Turns off runway for taxiway to terminal.
3. In reduced visibility misses turn onto main taxiway.
4. Inadvertently gets back onto runway in head to head position with next aircraft taking off -5.

Recommendation: Pay attention to headings when taxiing in very low visibility.

That same runway was plagued by the problem of aircraft landing on 22L that, after landing, would have to cross 22R to get to the terminal. I was number two for takeoff one night and watched Aer Lingus, who was number one, start his takeoff after being cleared to go—the earth shaking with the rumble of power as he pulled away from me. Holding off to the side was a 707 that had recently landed and was headed for the terminal. When Aer Lingus was well down the runway and going fast, the aircraft that was supposed to be holding started across the runway right in front of Aer Lingus! My heart stopped—it looked like a collision. Then Aer Lingus rotated, and I saw it stagger into the sky and just brush across the top of the 707 so close you couldn't tell if he missed or not. He missed.

The great part of it to me—and bless the Irish—came a few moments later when Aer Lingus called the tower and said, in a very calm voice rich with brogue, "That's a bit closer than I like it."

I never discovered the reason. When I took off after Aer Lingus I was headed for Hong Kong on a ten-day trip. When I got back I forgot to chase down the reason before I hurried off home.

The point is that even on a well-controlled airport the pilot should keep tabs on things and not blithely go along with everything the tower says without checking up on it and having a sense of responsibility about traffic and direction.

There's a part in the FAA's Air Traffic Control Data section, under Taxiing, a (5), that I'm going to quote, boring though it may be, because it's dynamite and an excellent example of when, despite rules, we have to be on top of what's going on.

When ATC clears an aircraft to "taxi to" an assigned takeoff runway, the absence of holding instructions authorizes the aircraft to "cross" all runways which the taxi route intersects except the assigned runway. It does not include authorization to "taxi onto" or "cross" the assigned take off runway at any point. In order to preclude misunderstandings in radio communications, ATC will not use the word "cleared" in conjunction with authorization for aircraft to taxi.

Almost amusingly the rule says, "in order to preclude misunderstandings . . ." but then promptly goes on to create them.

First it says ATC "clears" an aircraft to taxi, then, near the end of the rule, it says ATC will not use the word "cleared."

So how are you cleared without hearing the word "cleared"? It baffles me.

Of course, hanging such an important procedure on the use or not use of one word, especially thinking of the tumbling mass of words spilling out from a busy tower, is pretty unrealistic.

NASA says it loud and clear in its Technical Paper 1875, and I'm going to quote it because it's worthwhile. "Problems in the transfer of information within the aviation system were noted in over 70% of 28,000 reports submitted by pilots and air traffic controllers to the NASA Aviation Safety Reporting System (ASRS) during a five-year period 1976–1981."

So here is another place that pilot responsibility is critical: taxiing; it's no time to move without carefully looking down any runways to be crossed, even though the tower has said it's okay, even if they're supposed be inactive—they have a way of becoming active accidentally.

I don't want to dwell on this particular procedure for itself but rather because it exemplifies the fact that regulations, rules or procedures do not relieve the pilot of responsibility, and that in addition pilots should realize there are some regulations, rules or procedures that can dupe us into hazardous situations.

A smaller item about taxiing around an airport with big airplanes involves cutting the corner of a taxiway and clipping a light on the edge. The big jet airplanes have their rear wheels way back there, and it's easy to turn the nose, where everything looks all clear, toward a new direction, when actually the rear wheels are still back where we were. It's a good point worth remembering when transitioning to bigger airplanes. Don't press me on why I know about that one! The damage is generally small, except to one's ego.

Another point about taxiing is the yellow line. Theoretically if we keep the nosewheel on the yellow line our wing tips will clear other aircraft and buildings. Not so, because errors are made parking other aircraft, and sometimes that puts one in the path of your wing tip. An alert first officer, Ed Gardyan (later a captain), saved my hide as I was taxiing a 707 close to the terminal one rainy night when lights made vision a mass of reflections. He saw, at the last minute, that we were about to hit the wing of another 707 parked at the gate despite our being on the yellow line—the 707 had been parked wide. He called my attention to it, but it was so close and our collision imminent, he just went ahead and put on the brakes—we barely missed it.

Less Busy

Scaled down from the busy airport with a tower is the airport without a tower, but perhaps an FSS (Flight Service Station) that pilots call to give information as to their intentions, for all to hear. The FSS, in well protected legal words, advises pilots of the runway being used and what the *known* traffic is.

This is a paradoxical service; it enhances safety and is good, but if misinterpreted it can be dangerous. The FSS may tell us the runway being used, but there's nothing to prevent a pilot from arriving in the area and landing on a different runway—he may not bother to say so on his radio—he may not even have a radio. Our only protection is to use our eyes and remember the FSS is *not* a tower!

The traffic the FSS gives is only traffic known to it; there can be others around, the FSS knows nothing about. Sometimes I feel that we have to be more careful around FSS-equipped airports than ones without them. This in no way is to knock FSS people; they do a fine job, but they are buried away where, in most cases, they cannot even see the airport. They are at the mercy of people who may not call in. So it's up to us as we taxi out, or come into the airport to run our own show, and keep the FSS informed.

No Tower, No FSS

Then there's the airport with no tower. That's easier—it's all up to us. Making announcements via radio of our intentions and actions is an important part of this kind of flying, but this broadcasting doesn't relieve looking, constantly.

Unicom-equipped fields, in a way, fall into the same category as an FSS—unicoms are there for information, *not* to be a tower. Care has to be used when we are taxiing for takeoff not to taxi on the runway or area being used for landing—we've got to stay out of the way. Sometimes this is difficult because the takeoff-landing area on grass fields, with no runways, is not easy to define. This kind of operation demands taxiing at snail's pace, because who knows what unmarked holes or wet spots may be lurking ahead of us. Rough ground is most often the case, and being in a hurry can look silly—an example is the fellow I saw in a Skylane rushing down an airport headed for the runway and takeoff. He was going too fast for the rough area he was crossing. The nose of the Skylane bobbed up and down, and then I heard a "kling" sound as the propeller clipped the earth and a rock. He wasn't in a hurry anymore—there were prop repairs to make.

But the one that grinds me down is the habit I see demonstrated time and time again of pilots who taxi to the active runway for takeoff—on a no-tower airport—then swing into position for takeoff and sit there doing final checks, sometimes run-ups, for a long time before pouring on the coal and starting down the runway. He hasn't the slightest clue what's behind him—who may be landing over him! This is really a stupid practice. The last thing that must be done *immediately* before takeoff is to be in position or get in position to have a good look at the sky on the approach end of the runway.

This is the same type person who doesn't bother to see who's behind him at other times and blasts them. At Sugarbush two macho-piloted AT-6s came in for a Sunday show-off. When they left they turned sideways to the runway—good practice—while running up their engines, exercising props and making noise and confusion. The problem was they had turned their tails toward a parked glider—tied down, thank heaven—that strained at its ropes and tried everyway to get loose. It didn't, but the blast of dirt and small stones against its supersmooth wing's leading edge was damaging. Pretty dumb airmanship, fancy AT-6s and all.

Before we leave runways and taxiing it's worth mentioning that when holding near a runway's end for takeoff, waiting for an aircraft to land or take off, there is little point in holding too close to the runway—even close to the markings that signify the holding point. Now and then an airplane goes ape on landing, perhaps undershooting and getting mighty close to where we could be holding. If the holding point is parallel to the takeoff runway, a misguided takeoff also can make life precariously exciting.

Many things are observed while taxiing—checking that the directional gyros are turning as we turn, seeing that the turn and bank is too, making the important check that the controls are free with full travel, watching what the traffic is doing, the wind's action in direction, velocity and gusts—a host of things really. They fortify the case for a careful, slow, and *alert* attitude, the way the pros do it—the pilots I look up to.

The Italians have a wonderful expression that means to take it easy—I've used it lots in Rome's taxicabs: "Piano, piano." It goes well around airports too.

13

Takeoff

TAKEOFF is the exciting time, the end of planning, the start of ful-fillment—the tingling awareness that we're going to leave the earth and enter an element foreign to man but, indeed, wondrous. It's a time of abandonment, of unleashing power that makes speed increase to a level that at its peak, in a ground vehicle, would be difficult to control or stop. Instead, at the very height of what our inner self feels as approaching disaster, a gentle, velvet backward pull on the elevator ends the wildness. We leave the harsh ground and surrender to the smooth, secure feeling of a different ele-ment—the sky.

For more than fifty years I have pushed throttles forward from the humblest forty-horsepower Cub to the mighty Boeing 747, but never, in all the thousands of takeoffs, have I failed to feel that ex-citement and sense of adventure. Tomorrow, if I get out the 172 and go flying I know the feeling will come again.

Serious Business

But takeoff is a serious time that requires preplanning, aware-ness and precise flying—excitement and beauty may envelop us, but we still have to maintain a sense of cold calculation. Flying is rife with this tugging in different directions of our psyche, but it's part of the game. Some pilots may seem to be all calculation—computers that click without emotion or notice of the allurement surrounding them—but under there, somewhere, they feel it; they can stop, too, and seize the moment.

The real pro has it under control; he charges down the runway with all the thrill of takeoff, and feels it, is alive to it, but he's also watching the speed, knowing where V_1, the decision speed, is, how the power is set and all the rest.

Where It Starts

Takeoff starts when we open the throttles and begin our run, but where it ends can be argumentive. It seems that the end of takeoff is when the airplane is high enough so that our next action, in regard to trouble or the normal heading out on course, is no longer related to the ground close by.

I have to slip back to gliding for an example. When working thermals to climb or stay aloft, my attention, once I'm above some altitude—2,000 feet or so in the East where lift conditions are generally weaker than in the West—is on the sky above. I'm looking for clouds that tell of thermals, wisps of them that may be forming; watching old ones to see if they are disintegrating; checking the sky ahead to see if the cloud patterns are changing. Aside from a glance down now and then for navigation and checking terrain, I'm part of the sky.

But below that 2,000 feet my attention returns to the earth. What is the terrain like? Where may a thermal form? Is there a ridge that has lift, a field I could land in if I don't find lift? My mind is back to the ground.

And Ends

Takeoff is like that, and we haven't finished it until we are high enough, in a single engine, to have a choice of fields to use if the engine fails or, in a multiengine, to be able to clear obstructions in comfort should an engine fail; it's an altitude where we've finished tucking flaps away in a big jet and pulled the thrust back to climb value. So takeoff is all below that altitude.

We're not going into the details of speeds and the catechism of how it's done—that's up to good schools and instructors and manuals; what we want to talk about are some basics—as we're trying to do all along.

V_1

There is one detail we should talk about and that is V_1. We generally think of this number as the crossover point between taking off or aborting and stopping if trouble should crop up; before reaching V_1 speed we stop and after it we keep going.

There is a difference between a propeller airplane and a jet in this matter. Often the need to stop is more desperate in a propeller airplane because of the poor flying performance with an engine failed. A jet airplane has much better performance in this condition, and jet thrust is such that the power keeps increasing as speed increases. A piston doesn't do this.

The general run of commercial, municipal airports have runways of a length that give the propeller airplane more excess runway than jets have—runway to stop in.

Add to all this the unrealism of V_1 when the runway is wet or slick with snow or ice. It's often questionable if V_1 gives enough room to stop. It's a judgment call and a tough one because things are moving pretty fast and the decision has to be made now! Most flying decisions don't require a superquick response, and more people get in trouble moving too fast than too slow—V_1 is an exception.

Flying a jet, if the speed is on the high side, nearing V_1, chances are it's better to keep going and continue the takeoff than try to get her stopped. The record points to this, and there are numerous accidents, minor to major, that were caused when pilots tried to stop a jet from high speed. It's worth remembering that V_1 is an exact number, but the action connected with it is far from exact—another item firmly in the pilot's lap.

Legal

We will expect the airplane to be legal in weight and the runway sufficient considering wind, temperature, altitude, slope, slush and all those good things. On airlines this is computed with gnat's eye precision for each takeoff. It's not only a matter of safety, but economics too. They want to get the most allowable on board and still be invulnerable.

This care and concern isn't always demonstrated, however, in the world of general aviation, especially in light-twin operation, where cubic capacity is often confused with weight allowance; runway length is frequently judged as a matter of having enough room to get off without much thought about the consequences of an engine failure during this intense period.

Every person with a license, private to ATP (airline transport pilot), has been taught how to compute takeoff requirements and parameters under prevailing conditions. If, in spite of this knowledge, pilots take off when they are facing disaster should trouble occur, we can only put them in the category of dive and zoom people, those who skip preflights and the other simpletons of flying.

What Might Happen

Most concerns of takeoff are about things that may happen, and, I guess, it's safe to say that number one is engine failure. Beyond that comes a long list such as flaps not being down on an airplane that requires flaps for takeoff, spoilers being up on aircraft that have them, carburetor heat being on, fuel set on an empty tank or not on at all, wrong kind of fuel, tire blowing out, fire, aircraft taxiing across the runway, an aircraft from behind landing on the taking-off airplane—gosh, we could make up quite a list.

But to make certain we don't scare anyone let's agree that a good portion of the list is pretty farfetched—things that almost never happen; even the most obvious, an engine failure, is a very rare event. However, let's also recognize that while emergencies are rare they do happen on occasion, and because the event is infrequent, they may catch us flat-footed—fat, dumb and happy, as the old expression goes.

How do we protect against this rare occurrence—how do we bring ourselves up to peak performance from dreamy complacency in a split second? Well, let's talk about it.

First of all we observe that the reasons for takeoff trouble are often of our own doing: fuel valve set wrong, flaps forgotten, trim tabs way off and so on. The primary job, then, is to protect ourselves from ourselves.

Habit

The obvious way is a religious devotion to the use of checklists. However, checklists aren't in the 100 percent bracket, but let's set them aside for the moment and talk instead about habit patterns.

For instance, somewhere back in time I developed the habit of checking the gear down and locked when on final approach; even with the checklist all read, gear down and locked, I still cannot help but look at the green lights and double-check. Even when landing an airplane that doesn't have retractable gear, the feeling of checking it goes over me on final, and I've had quick little pangs reminding me that I hadn't put the gear down.

It seems that experienced pilots have a moment just before

takeoff and on approach to landing, when a quick thought goes through their mind saying, "Is everything set?" That seems to be a basic habit pattern, to make a final quick check.

How does one develop such patterns? I wish I could answer that, but it is in the realm of the psychologist—I often think it would pay a pilot to study psychology—law too.

This doesn't relieve, in any way, the use of the checklist—rather this is a double check of key terms. If we are certain of those key items we've relieved a big part of the problems—self-created—that might occur on takeoff—or landing.

Example: In a 747, ready to go, checklists read and responded to, I'm ready to advance the throttles, but by habit I look over my shoulder at the second officer's panel and glance at the fuel valves to see that they are set to the correct tanks, that fuel pumps are on and the fuel gauges showing about what the total fuel load should be; then, a look forward at the flap lever to be certain it's in the right position and at the spoiler handle, which I test with a push forward as my hand goes up to the throttles, a glance down to see that the stabilizer setting is within reason, and then all attention to the takeoff except a quick glance, as our eyes move toward the windshield, that checks to see if our heading information agrees with the runway heading.

Killer

This ritual takes perhaps three seconds, at the most five. But it covers what are grimly called "the killer items." If the fuel is on and enough fuel is in the tanks, there isn't going to be engine failure because of fuel starvation.

Fuel has to be getting to the power plant, a very key item, and in any airplane I'm flying—one I know or don't know—even riding as passenger in a G/A (general aviation) aircraft, I glance at the fuel valve and tank gauge as my pilot friend is starting takeoff.

In a piston engine the same glance goes by the oil pressure gauge. This is reinforced by an actual experience that didn't even get to takeoff. A friend was taking me up in his brand-new Cessna 180 he'd flown in from the factory the evening before. He was proud as punch. The engine started, and after it had I glanced around and noticed no oil pressure. I asked him if the new ship had different instruments, were they electrically operated—I was thinking we might not have a switch on—he answered no. I reached down and pulled the mixture control to kill the engine. He looked at me with a surprised, What the devil are you doing? look.

"No oil pressure." I hate people to do other people's action while flying; it's wrong and dangerous; but I thought quickness in cutting the engine might prevent damage, and that was more important than trying to explain it first—and besides we were parked on the ground near the hangar.

The reason was that after arriving from Wichita he'd asked that the oil be changed. It was, but only half. They'd drained it, then had a mechanic-shift change, the new people coming on didn't put any in, and I guess, he hadn't checked it! The running time was brief and I'm sure didn't harm the engine, but my friend never felt comfortable with that engine again.

Back to the killer items. Fuel on and proper, as we've said, removes a big part of the chance for engine failure. A look at flaps on an airplane that uses them on takeoff is important, because required runway length is affected—having full flaps down on many small airplanes could be serious trouble too. Spoilers extended can really reduce lift and raise hob with takeoff. It's amusing that we find spoilers on big jet airplanes and gliders—but no airplanes in between. (They are an excellent addition to aircraft control, and there are signs we may find them on small airplanes in the future—you can get them in kit form for a few types now, but not many have done it.)

Pushing forward on the spoiler handle to be certain they are re-tracted can be likened, on other airplanes, to pushing ahead on the propeller control to be certain it's in low pitch position for take-off. Fortunately we have developed an industry standard that says, "Everything forward for go." So prop controls forward, mixture controls forward (rich) and throttles too.

The important point is to develop a habit that makes us ask Is everything set? just before takeoff and landing. The object is to cover the killer items, but the list should be as short as possible. We can think it through carefully for the airplane we fly and de-cide the crucial items. Basically we're talking fuel to the en-gine(s) and the airplane configured so no aerodynamic degradation can occur at takeoff; the same for landing plus land-ing gear down. But, again, *in no way does this take the place of a checklist!* The habit is a short and quick check, a part of scan.

An important point before we roll is how close we're taking off after another aircraft, especially if it is a big one twirling vortices off its wing tips that will make us do snap rolls or other ungainly maneuvers of a kind highly dangerous when we're near the ground. Being close behind other airplanes has certain dangers on takeoff, landing and, in some cases, in the air. Fly through a DC-9's "wash" in a small airplane, and the jolt is frightening.

It's an important basic—that sorta says, "Being ahead is much better than being behind," or, "Be wary of horses' and airplanes' hind ends."

14

On the Roll

BACK A WAY we mentioned the importance of being able to leave the world of dreamy complacency and respond quickly and accurately to any demands on our flying that suddenly might appear.

Not difficult if we know what to do first, what realm of flight we're in and what it requires.

What to do first: As loud as it can be said and repeated a thousand times, "FLY THE AIRPLANE!"

Though we're surrounded by hell's fire and brimstone the airplane must be kept under control. Speed above stall and flown to stay that way leads the list; then we worry about turning, climbing, descending or whatever is needed. If it's a multiengine with an engine out, keeping control in relation to stall is number one, but close behind it is keeping the lateral and directional control under the asymmetric condition.

The next plateau is knowing what we need to do for the flight realm we're working in and nowhere does this apply more aptly than during takeoff.

Speeds

Knowing the proper speeds for the various segments of takeoff gives us a number to shoot for and hold on to, whether for a normal departure or abnormal—such as having an engine out.

We're not going into a long dissertation about emergencies here—we did that in the book, *Flying Know-How*. What we'd like to get across now is that there are very exact numbers to fly by, and one should have them firmly in mind so that in saying, "fly the airplane," a person knows what numbers to shoot for—what airspeeds.

In earlier days, before well-defined numbers came into use, pilots made takeoffs and climbs to their liking, dictated by pet theories. One group argued you should hold 'er down and get lots of speed and then climb out, others said to climb out at high rate and get up and away from everything. One group pulled the airplane off at the slowest speed, others let it gather speed on the ground, bouncing and jarring, before they jerked it into the air.

As aircraft performance increased, as more sophisticated wings came into being, it became evident that more precise ways of flying the airplane were needed to get the most benefit from these advances. We started the numbers game, and it's a good game.

The pilot who argued that it was best to get off and climb away from the earth quickly was on the right track, but he lacked preciseness, his theory needed refinement. Now this has been done—computed by engineers, aerodynamicists and pilots to exact numbers.

The old grumble that went something like "engineers don't know what's goin' on in the real world" has gone into the mists of the past. I've worked in the flight-test and performance sections of major manufacturers—the talent there will humble you. Almost any test pilot is a graduate engineer, well programmed in that discipline as well as in aerodynamics; he works closely with other engineers and aerodynamic specialists who, you will find, also know a lot about flying. The test pilot will often be the person in charge of the entire program of testing, licensing and performance of a new aircraft.

It's been my good fortune to have worked with these people in their offices, walled off by glass partitions from acres of open spaces, bright with a multitude of fluorescent lights and filled with drawing boards, desks and engineers; to have been with them in computer rooms; to have flown in simulators dedicated to research and testing. So it's kind of a shock to leave that atmosphere with the person you've been conferring with at a desk, a serious type with shirt and tie, and walk through the factory to the ramp, climb in an airplane and fly a series of stalls. It's a thought-provoking adjustment; this guy shouldn't be able to fly an airplane! He's a businessman! Where are his leather jacket, his piercing blue eyes speculating with wisdom on what the sky has to tell, his attitude of restrained talk? It's gone. The person you're walking with may have brown eyes, be exuberant about some aspect of the flying we're about to do, and as you find out once in the airplane, is one very superior airman.

Numbers

It isn't a segregated business any more; there aren't just engineers, or aerodynamicists, or pilots; they are all one, and they know what they are doing. The numbers that finally come to us, via manuals where this knowledge and effort wind up, are the right ones, and if we believe them and fly them we can do no better—most likely if we don't we'll do a lot worse.

The numbers aren't done once and then forgotten either. Continuing tests and refinements go on for the life of the airplane as it's improved and modified. A good manufacturer updates information to the user. Boeing still investigates better ways to fly the

727, for example, and its design is over twenty years old.

Now we're ready to fly; we know what airspeeds we'll go for. In a multiengine airplane we have minimum control speed well in mind, as well as V_1, V_R, V_2. We're flying the airplane to those numbers, and that's where we go when we talk about "flying the airplane." In a single, small airplane we've decided whether we want to climb out at best angle or best rate and picked the airspeed the book says to use for either one: V_x or V_y. There's a best speed for gliding with total power loss. Speeds to cover all situations are in the manual, and knowing them one knows how to fly the airplane under any condition.

This points to two things; one is knowing the manual well and how to compute or look up any speed that's needed, particularly when flying in marginal conditions of runway length, load, temperature and the other factors that limit performance.

The second point is to have these speeds well in mind in advance so if something occurs out of the norm we know instantly how to fly the airplane—to what speed. It, again, is planning and being ahead.

Actually this speed concept, this method, has made flying simpler. It takes away a certain scrambled confusion of thoughts that interfere with the work of managing the aircraft, maneuvering within the ATC system and responding to weather demands. For flying, the numbers are there; all we have to do is maintain them; for normal best climb or for struggling with an engine out, the manual speed will give us the best chances to climb, to clear obstructions or whatever.

One note of caution: If you have an excess of speed over the speed called for, be miserly giving it up. Example: Multiengine takes off, has a power failure because an engine fell off, seriously affecting the airplane's flying qualities; at this point the airspeed is above the engine-out climb speed, but having V_2 as the speed to fly with an engine-out drilled into him during training and checking, the pilot reduces his speed back to V_2. But the damaged airplane can't be controlled at the slower speed. Had he maintained the higher speed and not given it away, the airplane, studies showed, could have been flown; instead it crashed.

This isn't criticism of the pilot—this was a way-out situation and he did what he'd been taught, but it demonstrates that one needs judgment and analysis in any condition even though the numbers are the way to fly, and sometimes we can use a little luck too.

This is a kind of Monday-morning quarterbacking we don't like to do, because sometimes there just isn't enough time and the situation is too complex to make an analysis and come up with the proper action. Then it's back to "fly the airplane," at the numbers, and hope it all turns out okay—most times it does.

Flaps

Another matter, flaps. Many high-performance airplanes have to use flaps for takeoff. They make airplanes fit in runways that would be impossible without flaps. Flaps change the wing section, change its C_L and, in many cases, add area. They help with lift, but we pay for it with drag, and that's the reason the airplanes are "cleaned up"—flaps retracted—within the earliest sensible period after takeoff: to get rid of that drag and establish a sparkling climb rate.

Whether or not an airplane needs flaps for takeoff is well spelled out in its manual. But we do have a problem with airplanes that don't require flaps for takeoff—small singles generally.

The manual will say that the use of flaps gets the airplane off the ground quicker—a help in getting it up out of mud, snow, gravel and such—but once in the air the climb deteriorates.

A quote from the Cessna 172 manual makes the point. "The

use of 10° flaps will shorten the ground run approxiamtely 10%, but the advantage is lost in the climb to a 50-foot obstacle.''

The doubtful action is people making takeoffs using flaps when they don't have to—when, in some cases, they would be better off—better able to clear an obstacle farther away—if flaps hadn't been used.

The 2,600-foot runway here at Sugarbush, Vermont, is a good example. There are no immediate obstructions, but a mile or so south there are some hills you'd like to get up and over. It's a time to take off without flaps, to quickly get in the best climb condition and gain altitude over those hills. But the frequent occasions when you see flaps used on airplanes that don't require them for takeoff seem to prove that some pilots haven't read the manual enough to understand the facts. It isn't a thing to dwell on, but the point has enough importance to remind us that in some situations using flaps could introduce a hazard in that the clearance of certain obstructions might be degraded rather than improved.

Some pilots may get fancy ideas about using flaps on takeoff and then retracting them soon after getting in the air—very low. This is a dicey business and not recommended—it also requires a gentle hand and experience.

Of course there's the chance flaps might be retracted inadvertently, and we ought to know how to handle that. A gentle tug back on the wheel will generally do it. Flaps down, we're getting extra lift; a sudden raising of the flaps and we lose the extra lift. We well know that lift is increased by going to a higher alpha— angle of attack. We do this by pulling back, but gently because we are in a high lift condition, not very far from stall—if we're ham handed and haul back abruptly, we could get into stall territory with lift loss and drag increase.

Actually pulling back as flaps go up can be felt, so that we pull back just enough—not much is needed—to keep the airplane from sinking. It's a place where feel plays an important part: feel of acceleration and of what your eyes see—whether settling or holding your own.

I had this happen in a dramatic way during World War II, taking off in a C-54 (DC-4) from Marrakech, Morocco, for Prestwick, Scotland, very heavy with fuel because it was a long trip with a big detour west over the Atlantic to avoid Europe, which then was held by the unfriendly folks. The gear and flap levers were low on the pedestal and much alike. We ran down the rough, unfinished runway and hauled the airplane into the air early to avoid the beating it was taking. Once airborne, "Gear Up!" was called, but by error the flaps were raised instead! You could immediately feel and see the airplane sink toward the ground—but a gentle pull back kept it flying, albeit not very briskly. The pull back was nervously done because we were very high on the lift curve due to load and forcing the airplane in the air—and we were very low. It was a tense moment, but worked out okay. Today it probably wouldn't happen because we fly precise numbers—at that time we were approaching the concept but not yet there; now the airport would be paved and long enough; in modern airplanes, the gear and flap lever are distinguished from each other by shape and they are located farther apart in the cockpit, although exact locations haven't been standardized in G/A aircraft—so we should "think" before we move a lever and not just use knee-jerk action.

This need for careful flying can occur on a go-around or aborted landing. It's worth practicing—up at a safe altitude—if it's not in your bag of tricks now.

Let's Go

Now we're at the end of the runway, the real end and not part way down it; we're cleared for takeoff or satisfied no one is on approach—the way is clear. We have in mind the numbers; we've finished the checklist and made our personal Is everything set? glance—we might as well open the throttles and go.

Apply the Power

There's a way to open throttles; we have to remember that the numbers and runway-length requirements are based on getting the power on and not dawdling about the job. Of course it's not good practice to slam on power, especially on a piston engine, but the engine can take a brisk, smooth acceleration, and that's what we ought to give it, because if we take a longish time to achieve take-off power, our runway values are going to pot—we're effectively shortening the runway.

We should use all the power allowed. The engine is certified for max takeoff power, the runway distance is computed using it, so why not? It's false safety not to use max power when called for.

I checked a captain one time during Connie days who thought he'd save engines by taking off at far less than takeoff power. The airplane used a major portion of the runway and put him in a position that if he'd had an engine failure his obstruction-clearance buffer would have been seriously jeopardized. He argued strongly when this was pointed out to him, and I'm sure that once he was alone and not being checked, being an individualist, went right on doing it his way. (We finally got him brainwashed when he checked out in jets.)

Airlines do use reduced takeoff thrust on jets to lower engine wear, but the lesser thrust is computed for the runway being used and the conditions, so all safety margins are maintained. Taking off in bad weather, gusty winds or marginal runways, however, full thrust is used—or any time the captain decides he wants it.

The takeoff run is a PHC—Period of High Concentration. We keep the airplane straight; check that the power is set properly;

watch to see we're accelerating, that everything is operating normally, getting ready to reach the rotation airspeed, thinking what
airspeed we'll fly in climb and telling ourselves the heading and
altitude we're going for once we're airborne; there's a memory
reference to the frequency we'll have to change to when in the air;
thinking when, in a flapped airplane, we'll start increasing speed
to begin flap retraction; if it's a noise abatement takeoff, what
procedure we'll follow, such as the brisk left turn after takeoff
from runway 31L at JFK; then departure SID (Standard Instrument Departure)—go to Bridge—make sure to turn east of Canarsie's 039 radial—cross JFK's 253 at or above 2,500—maintain
5,000; double-check the ADF is tuned to Bridge, Number 1 omni
to Canarsie, Number 2 to JFK.

All that and more, but what's the key item—small airplane or
big? Rotate at the proper speed and then go for the climb-out airspeed.

"V_R—Rotate!"

Rotation demands a little attention—the matter of how one
pulls back at takeoff. It should be a firm, positive, smooth pressure. Too quick, and the airplane is jerked into the sky, perhaps
roughly enough so alpha becomes high and drag increases. Too
slow, however, and it takes the airplane more distance to become
airborne, and the runway length, effectively, is shortened—we
use more of it—and our obstacle clearance at the end is reduced.
This, of course, is for jets of all kinds that are likely to have situations where runways are just about adequate—it doesn't mean
much for a 150 horsepower single-engine airplane departing on a
4,000-foot runway! But even that airplane has its days operating
from marginal runways when correct rotation is necessary.

The "book" once said that performance was based on the pilot
pulling back so the airplane's nose raised at a rate of 3° per sec-

ond. This was impractical to measure, and airplanes at different acceleration rates demand slightly different rotation techniques— so now it's pretty much pilot judgment that tells you fairly well if you are under- or over-rotating. Anyway, the idea is not to rotate so slowly valuable runway is wasted, or so fast too high an alpha is reached, with increased drag or worse. It all comes back to being smooth and positive. And this is a good time to point out that to be smooth we don't have to be slow—the two do not necessarily equate.

We're Off

But now we've rotated and are off—scanning seriously, coming back frequently to the ADI to see that the left turn has proper bank and not increasing or decreasing—that the nose attitude is about where it should be for the climb speed we want. We're thinking a lot of things, but doing it in order, first things first, and flying the airplane is first. Speed—attitude—altitude—heading; our eyes frequently catching the ADI, making certain it's not going way off—if it isn't, we aren't.

Sounds busy and it is, but not that busy; a mind moves very quickly, takes in a lot in an instant as long as we don't befuddle it, as long as we have things organized in their proper order. I was surprised to find you're not really rushed in a supersonic F-104 fighter even though it only takes about three minutes to get to 41,000 feet! But any airplane, fast, slow, small or big, is worked the same way: first to be certain it's flying, then for performance, altitude, navigation and radio reporting, which certainly should be toward the last.

That's normal takeoff, but what if there's trouble? Then the priorities are more clear-cut—simpler. Fly it! All else is secondary. Naturally you try to keep an element of order in respect to traffic and communications, but these things shouldn't clutter the mind and degrade the way we fly the airplane. If we know well the speeds and attitudes for various conditions such as an engine out—or even glide speed with no power at all—the battle is 90 percent won.

Why are the calm, cool pilots that way? Because they know the numbers and they have a firm sense of priorities.

Bad Weather

Many takeoffs are made into bad weather—or black holes at night—they add something extra.

First, if it's weather, we have to be certain the airplane is set up for the weather at hand: anti-icing equipment on if needed, radar sweeping the sky if we'll be getting into thunderstorms—pretty cut and routine stuff, but important.

The aspect we want to talk about, most, however, is the transition from visual to instrument flight, and that's why we said black hole as well as bad weather. Taking off from Shannon, Ireland, at night toward the river: A long run, lift off and about then the end of the runway flashes by and you are out over the river—effectively it is suddenly zero-zero, no reference—you might as well have a sack pulled over your head. Except, of course, there are instruments, and immediately we go to them to climb out; pitch attitude and wings level. Forget the earth—it's gone, and there's no use worrying about it or trying to keep it in view. If we have the power and attitude required for climb there's no worry about flying back into the ground—we are climbing and doing it the safest way.

There is great hazard for inexperienced pilots, who may not have their instrument ratings, not understanding that taking off at night, even a sparkling clear night, into a black area like the river at Shannon or the empty country around their local airport, can be just as much an instrument-flying task as climbing into a cloud layer.

Perhaps even worse is taking off and going out over sparsely settled country with scattered lights. Trying to fly visually, look-ing at a few lights, may give illusions, causing subtle disorienta-tion that can result in flying into the ground without even realizing it. It is especially a time to cross-check instruments—attitude and altitude.

Lots of VFR-only pilots fly at night, but there are many lights, or a moon or a sky bright enough to give a horizon of sorts. It's near the ground, when we are in the pitlike region of darkness, that our reference is distorted or disappears, and we are indeed flying in danger.

It is the classic time when instruments are paramount; they have no illusions; they give precise, hard facts, and we should go to them for security. If we do not have the ability to fly by instru-ments then our limits should exclude most night flying and cer-tainly instrument flying, particularly when marginal weather is combined with darkness.

What about taking off in dense fog—zero, zero? Not smart. We need some visibility. It may only be a few centerline lights or a distinct painted line down the middle of the runway. But you need some visual guidance to get started.

Before ever starting such a gambit we should have been lined up and certain our gyros are all up to speed. Equally important—perhaps more so—is that *we* are up to speed, meaning expert in the instrument-flying department.

As we accelerate, the visual reference goes by faster and faster and finally fast enough to be difficult to use—or we may suddenly run into an area down the runway that is London Fog zero, zero, and we cannot see anything! Then it's all attention on the heading and, when rotation airspeed is reached, pulling back and going for climb-out attitude. It's like the black hole and going completely on instruments and forgetting about the ground, except you do it sooner.

The dicey part is when only using instruments during the

ground roll. Everything has to be perfect: airplane lined up to start with, gyros up to speed, pilot perfect. Yes, perfect, because there's only the runway width for error, and that isn't enough to be safe.

Try this under the hood, a standing start, with a pilot friend along to keep you out of trouble, and you'll find it's tough to stay on the runway and not go off to one side. The real answer is that takeoffs just shouldn't be made unless one is certain there will be enough visibility to keep on the runway visually during the take-off roll. Also, even with some visual guidance, it's a 100 percent instrument task the moment you start to raise the nose. The limited visual reference disappears under the nose as soon as the nose begins to come up because it cuts off the short range forward view; we're on instruments and the rear wheels haven't even left the ground!

So no matter what's legal or not, good judgment says these kinds of takeoffs shouldn't be attempted unless we have some visibility and we are very experienced instrument pilots.

Attitude

During these dissertations we frequently refer to using attitude, to attain the airspeed we want by checking attitude. Any experienced pilot knows what we're talking about; flying attitude is the basic way instruments are flown.

We don't rotate on takeoff and then start chasing the airspeed we want to fly; we know that at takeoff power a certain attitude will give us proper climb-out speed or close to it. When we pull back on the wheel of a Boeing 747 for takeoff our eyes go to the ADI and rotate until a pitch attitude of 15° is reached; that's where we climb out. The airspeed will fall close to the one we want; for my Cessna 172, the number is about 7°; in the glider, circling in a thermal, the position of the nose in relation to the horizon will give me close to the speed I want with just a glance, now and then, at the airspeed indicator to fine-tune it. In other words, we don't chase the airspeed indicator; we set a pitch and then see what value the speed settles on—if it's a tad slow we use a little less pitch attitude—if fast, we use a little more nose up. In an airplane we fly a lot, the attitudes are almost known by heart.

Attitude is used in roll, too, for amounts of turn and for other maneuvers—no wonder we check the ADI so often.

That's attitude flying, and most people reading this know how to use it—if you don't, get a good instrument instructor to show you how; it's as much a part of flying as the controls.

15

Climb Out

HAVING A PLAN or an ATC clearance we know where we're headed as we climb; we also know what airspeed to fly. What's to do? Look!

Collision is the problem, and most collisions occur within five or so miles of an airport; they aren't reserved for VFR flying or uncontrolled airplanes; they occur with one or both airplanes on flight plans, under control, on or off instruments and mostly under 10,000 feet.

It all says something; watch out—outside, that is. Getting settled, checking a map or departure plate, making notes tends to make people forget to look out while climbing. Airlines have paper work. Recorded on every airline departure and arrival are the times *o*ut from the gate, *o*ff the ground, *o*n the ground and *i*n the gate—called O-O-O-I times—pronounced "ooo-ee." The first or second officer writes them down and along with other information transmits them to the company ground station. This is done during climb when the crew member ought to be looking out the window!

In fairness, some airlines say, "No paper work during climb and descent!" although they generally don't reduce paper work requirements to follow up the order. A better way is a gadget called ACARS (Arinc Communications Addressing and Reporting System) that automatically records these times and telemeters them back to the ground without the crew member doing a thing. These are being installed by airlines that can afford them, but it will be a long time before everyone has the equipment—heads-down cockpit paper work will be around for years to come, so don't always expect an airliner to see you.

The rest of us can do our best to make the climb period a time for looking out. We may use a pad to scratch down our time and fuel at takeoff, but why can't we can remember these numbers until we level off at cruise and then write them down.

VFR?

Even though we're on an instrument flight plan, under ATC control, we're not protected from all traffic, and the mixture of VFR traffic and controlled IFR traffic in the same airspace means everybody has to look outside.

While we may be on an instrument flight plan, under control, there is much of the time that we're not actually on instruments, but on top, between layers or in clear sky. That's when VFR traffic may be in the same airspace with IFR, and we need to keep a sharp eye. ATC's radar doesn't always pick up VFR traffic; they may warn you of some, but they'll miss many. It hasn't been infrequent that an airplane zips by unannounced—you call ATC and ask what that was. They come back saying they haven't anything showing. Also there are those immortal words written in various ATC papers regarding VFR aircraft and radar—they say, "Radar advisories on all unidentified aircraft are provided on a work-load permitting basis." That's quoted from Allentown, Pennsylvania, tower letter to airmen No. 84-02. They are words that get "them" off the hook. So don't expect coverage that may not be there.

One afternoon coming into JFK from Europe, descending through 6,000 feet, I passed a Cherokee head to head. It wasn't a near miss by any means, but close enough to identify. Being in a Terminal Control Area the Cherokee should have been under control. I called and asked why I hadn't been told of this traffic. The response: "He's VFR, and that's handled by a controller on the other side of the room!" A few days later I went up to the IFR room to see for myself and sure enough—almost lonesome, there was the VFR controller with scope, off by himself, out of current contact with the other controllers! I hope that's been changed since.

When VFR is marginal the responsibility for a sharp lookout from aircraft under ATC control is even more important. The weather limits of VFR are numbers, but—your idea of what a required three miles looks like and my idea may be very different; looking into the sun under hazy conditions can turn three miles into zero. Then, heaven forbid, there's the cheater, the one who spirals down through a small hole that's illegal, or climbs through one to get on top—there are all kinds of possibilities. The unsatisfactory answer is that we have to look, and there's no flight control that gives complete protection—the closest you'll come to it is flying high over the North Atlantic, and other oceans, where everything is under control and other kinds of traffic just aren't around.

Fortunately most flying folks are responsible and try to stick by the rules. They also use good sense and work on the basis of staying out of busy traffic areas unless necessary—I have no desire to fly my 172 into JFK, as well as I know the airport.

Total Control Isn't Necessary

I don't believe in controlling all the airspace and requiring flight plans everywhere—we do very well with our present system. Pilots should have flying freedom—to me that is what VFR means—Free Flying. In having it we VFR users well realize there has to be control and restrictions in some areas—busy terminals and such—but it's a big sky, a wide land and shutting all that off to Free Flying—VFR—would be senseless.

But this freedom, like all freedoms, requires a certain responsibility—in this case to fly by the rules. It is important to remember that the rules, by nature, are inadequate and always will be because you cannot be precise in judging visibility vis-à-vis distances or predict what the weather will do 100 percent of the time. So part of the responsibility is the use of honest judgment. There's no special trick in knowing when the conditions we're flying in don't provide enough vision to see another aircraft. When this is the case we have to do something about it such as getting out of there or calling ATC to file a flight plan. Being legal or not isn't the question—common sense is!

So to risk boring by repetition—any time we can see beyond the nose we should scan the sky as much as possible, regardless of IFR or VFR and especially in climb!

Surrounding Terrain

Takeoffs aren't always made in good weather, or daylight. At night or in poor weather we cannot see hilly terrain around the area. It is very necessary, of course, to miss the terrain. Will our flight path assure us of that? If there is an instrument-departure procedure published for the airport can we follow it and feel protected from terrain? Generally, yes, but don't always count on it. Some airlines, for example, have gone beyond the official procedures and established more conservative flight paths because they weren't comfortable with the published ones under all conditions.

So if airlines don't accept all the procedures, we as itinerants or infrequent users may not want to either. Our climb rate could be lots slower under heavy load, high temperatures or the effects caused by wind flowing down the mountain slopes, or bouncing off them, to create downdrafts that make climbing difficult.

What do we do? Study the charts; ask the locals; see if there's an alternate climb route that will take us away from the terrain until we are high enough to clear it all and turn back on course. The main point is to be aware of the possible problem and then use good sense to work it out.

Climb Speed

After the initial takeoff climb is completed and we're settled into a steady climb, what speed do we want? It's a matter of winds aloft and flight plan, the kind of thing we do in advance. If there's a big tail wind aloft we like to get up there and benefit from it, so our climb speed will be at a best rate; if it's head winds increasing all the way up, we may use a so-called cruise climb, which is at a higher speed.

These are the kinds of things to work out on cold winter nights by the fire with the airplane manual in hand and a calculator: a time to work out different hypothetical flights and see what's best. There's no better way to learn the airplane and its performance than exercises like that. It beats rules of thumb picked up in bull sessions. Working it yourself, with the manual, gives hard numbers to count on. Airplanes are different; a small single may have a best-operating altitude of 7,000 feet, a jet's will be way up high and very sensitive to load. Manuals have a wealth of information, the place you find the answers. They are worth study and are better than reading a lot of books and expecting magic answers—it's fun too.

A small point when one is climbing in a long-nosed airplane like some of the twins: The long nose, at best rate-of-climb speed, sticks up in the air in front of our vision path, so for seeing's sake it is best to climb at a higher airspeed that results in a lower nose

position. If we don't want to do that, then a wandering climb so
we can survey the sky ahead—like taxiing a tail dragger—is
necessary.

Level Off

Finally we reach the top of climb and level off. Most important, if we're on an instrument flight plan, is to remember what
altitude we've been cleared to and are supposed to fly. It's
surprising how often pilots "dope off" and climb right through
the altitude ATC cleared them to. There are altitude-warning devices on most airline and corporate aircraft that let you know by
an audio sound and light when you're approaching the altitude—
provided you set the altitude in the warning gadget when ATC
gives you a clearance. It's an excellent piece of equipment to
have, but not infallible.

How do we level off? On the altitude, but leave climb power on
until cruise-indicated airspeed is reached, then pull back to cruise
power setting. Lots of folks think that to get "on the step" you
have to go above the cruise altitude a few hundred feet and then
make a shallow dive to get speed and be on the "step."

All a fallacy. There isn't any "step." For a certain weight and
power the airplane will fly level at a certain alpha and that's that.
The climbing above and diving to get speed does the same thing
as leaving climb power on, at the exact altitude, until the airplane
accelerates to cruise speed. The difference is that in going above
cruise altitude for the dive we're working toward other traffic at
the next higher level. Someone says, "Come on, what's a few
hundred feet." Not much unless the airplane above is sloppily
flying a few hundred feet low, or there's an altimeter error—
which isn't impossible if you are set to local area pressure and the
other pilot hasn't gotten around to that yet and is still using an altimeter setting obtained in another area. Or an airplane coming

down from high altitude where all are on 29.92 inches of mercury hasn't had its altimeter reset to local station pressure (QNH) after descending below 18,000 feet—not an uncommon error. This can work in reverse, of course, when an altimeter isn't set to 29.92 inches after climbing above 18,000.

Little errors added together make big ones—serious ones. It makes a strong case for flying as precisely as possible.

16

Cruise

CRUISE IS a time of management, and like most management it differs with the kind of person doing the managing.

What does that mean? Simply that some people visualize cruise as that long boring period until you near the destination and descend, while others think of it as a time to get a lot done, a time of minimum pressure to use for keeping ahead of the airplane and enjoying what's around.

I'm often asked if I didn't find flying the ocean boring; weren't the long hours filled with ennui? No, they were not; there was much to do: be certain of the navigation, gather weather, think of it in relation to the rest of the flight and particularly the destination—looking at weather constantly to see if its changes would give an opportunity to fly the flight better—other altitudes for improved winds, temperatures or smooth air; careful checking of the airplane's systems and power plants for their condition; monitoring fuel burn; recording the actual weather against the forecast so you could give the meteorological people on the other end an idea of what the weather had really been; thinking about making schedule although that falls in last after the operational and safety items. Then there were little experiments you'd work with that related to weather or airplane performance; communication and listening to other flights ahead, behind, or to the side to check how they were doing for information that might be helpful in better management of your flight. Cruise a boring time? Only if you make it that way.

I find it no different in a small airplane on a simple VFR flight; the protective curiosity is always there, the inquisitiveness.

Navigation

So let's dissect some of this and start with navigation.

There are a lot of different kinds of navigation available in the sky today, from dead reckoning with compass and map to a fancy inertial navigation system (INS). What you have, generally, is what you can afford.

No matter how basic or sophisticated, however, there's one fundamental, important to all navigation. Simply, that it's a science of suspicion—suspicion because good navigation is being suspicious of your position enough so that you keep checking to make certain where you think you are is really where you are.

When you are dead reckoning by compass and map: The bridge down there that crosses that river with the bend in it near the town—is that where we are or do other places along the river look the same; is there another setup farther along that's much like this one? That's an interesting point about dead reckoning and map reading, you generally think you're farther ahead than you are. If a setup doesn't measure up as it should, doesn't look quite right, look back along the course first, rather than farther along. I guess it's our eagerness to go faster, get there, that keeps us thinking we're ahead of our actual position.

Then to the sophisticated extreme, using inertial: Are the coordinates in the computer correct—have any numbers been transposed; are the way points in correct sequence; is the autopilot really in the inertial mode?

These things aren't checked once and then forgotten—no, they need rechecking, frequent checking because events along the way can create distraction, a miss-motion may have moved the wrong lever or pushed a button, the reciprocal used instead of the bearing—and so on.

Is this frantic, very time consuming? No, it isn't frantic or time consuming—it's relaxed. The careful review keeps things snug and flowing smoothly—that keeps the atmosphere relaxed.

Navigation is made up of a number of different things and is a fascinating art. The tasks are these: knowing position, then knowing what to do with it; how to correct for the course we want to make good, compute speed and Estimated Time of Arrival (ETA).

Position

Let's talk about knowing position; one key to that is to know position from the start. If we check position against the track we want, early after takeoff, we quickly sense if we're not going as we should; then corrections can be made and things set straight before we're well along and, perhaps, far off course and lost to some degree.

In a way it's like scanning when we check the ADI for pitch and roll attitude to be certain the airplane is flying as we want it. With navigation we check position to know if we're flying down the track we want. If we check frequently we never get far off. There's an old saying somewhere that most pilots who get lost get lost right after takeoff.

These cautions apply to any type of navigation system, and just because it's sophisticated and computerized doesn't mean we cannot stray far off with it. It's simply that the reasons are different, but in the final analysis no system is error free! With compass and map we can make mistakes in plotting, or the wind we planned for is different from that forecast; using INS we can program the computer improperly, or manage the system wrongly.

How to spot these errors? Scan and double-check that our numbers and procedures are correct for one. But finding and knowing our position is the ultimate test. If we're not on course there's something wrong.

Early 747 days—depart Paris for New York, fly across France and leave the coast not far from Brest. The INS was doing the work, all the way points filled in and the autopilot flying. The INS light came on saying we had ten miles to Quimper, the final fix on the French coast before starting across the sea. We passed over, the way point changed and the INS told the autopilot where to steer the airplane. But when the change occurred it seemed to me that we made a pretty hefty left turn. I checked the compass heading, and it was too far south for the next point. I reached down and checked the way point program in the computer—yes, it said we were headed toward 48°00′N-07°00′W. The first officer checked his—yes, it was okay—the second officer checked too, okay. I was baffled. Perhaps we'd put in the wrong coordinates at Orly Field when we set up the INS at the gate—Paris is east longitude, it could be easy to miss that and put west instead. But our time and distance to Quimper had been right on the nose, so we couldn't have made that mistake at Orly. "Okay, let's all check this again, carefully." We did, number by number, and there it was—47°00′N-08°00′W. We had the right numbers, but in the wrong places! Our first quick check—three of us—had seen the "right" numbers, but we'd missed the sequences. We reprogrammed and went on our way, with a big lesson learned—from then on I had a new double check procedure. But that's what sort of errors can be lurking in the computer world.

Basics

Whether we fly with sophisticated equipment or compass and map, basic navigation principles are needed in our background. Those early lessons plotting courses and applying variation were important. A pilot needs, well implanted in his mind, the picture of maps with course lines and what direction is, what a compass does and the difference betweeen the north pole and the magnetic pole—variation.

We need to develop an almost instinctive feeling for direction. The old tale that some have a sense of direction and some do not has been pretty well disproved. People who seem to have a good sense of direction are people more observant than those who don't. One kind automatically makes a mental note of which way they're going when starting out—others blithely depart without paying attention or giving even a tiny thought about direction. Pilots get like that too—take off, turn to a heading and fly along watching the sights until sometime later when they begin to wonder where they are; most times they don't know.

Maps

Maps. Basics again. Learn maps, how to read them, interpret them, feel them; be able to glance at them and quickly relate what's on the paper to what's below. Learn distances and scale, and terrain features such as mountains, rivers, oceans.

My early copilot days I was teamed with Captain Dick Hanson flying New York to Kansas City. On the first trip Hanson said to me, "In one month I'll expect you to know every town between Newark and Kansas City!" Panic.

I glued together maps of the route, cut and folded to make a map book, and then I studied it, not only at home, but every instant in the air, when it was open on my lap. At month's end Hanson would point to a group of lights below, only a few, shaped like the outline of a horse, "What's that?"

"Hickory"—Hickory, Pennsylvania. He didn't ask big places like Fort Wayne, but little ones. It was the days of poor radio reception—no VHF, but four course ranges that went out in a crackle of noise when it snowed or thunderstorms were around—even during rain some of the time. It was important when there was a break in the clouds, just a glimpse at the earth through a hole, to know where it was—and you were.

Forty-seven years later I still fly with a map handy, much of the time in my lap. It's not only been helpful, from DC-3 to jet, but it has added knowledge to life and romantic curiosity about the world. Knowing maps well also adds to the craftiness of a pilot; we are quicker, when glancing at a map, to recognize the peculiar twist of a coast line, the quick rise of mountains from a plain, the particular pattern of certain lakes, the fact that a mountain airport, down in a valley, will have one tough approach because of a ridge close to it.

The story maps tell never ends, and it's too bad more pilots don't use them. The tendency today is to have the radio facility charts take their place. But radio charts show where omnis are, radio beacons, various radio aids—few other features. Too many pilots are flying on course—out an omni radial—but don't know where they are. What happens if an engine quits? Where is that nearest airport? If we'd been following the map, even in a cursory fashion, we'd know.

There are three basic principles of flight that my friend Captain Walt Moran expounds—with his sly Irish smile: "Avoid the terrain, be patient, and never carry a bundle by the string." Deep stuff and not as comic as it may seem. But putting maps and Walt's first principle together—how are you going to avoid the terrain if you don't know how high it is? Maps, reading maps, following where we are by map reference, learning the elevations from them so if things are desperate—we unexpectedly get on instruments, or off course—we know what altitude to scamper to and "avoid the terrain."

A worthwhile exercise is occasionally to make a cross-country flight by dead reckoning alone—leave the navigation radios off, go from A to B by compass and map. I've often wondered how airline pilots, who are vectored into position on every airport, for almost every landing, would fare if suddenly radar was done away with and they had to find the airport and end of the runway on their own. Oh, they'd find it, but there would be a bit of wandering and wondering before they did. A highly impractical idea, of course; imagine the delays and utter chaos that would reign—for many reasons.

The exercise of flying without radio is a good one for practice, for fun and a return to the feeling that we are real pilots who can make it on our own if need be—without all that fancy help.

Celestial

Stars—celestial navigation: almost dead, the victim of technological advancement. Who needs star sights and fixes with INS or Omega, VLF, Loran and a future of satellites? Few if any. I miss celestial even though it was what I like to call historic navigation. You took a three-star fix, and it told you where you had been five or ten minutes ago depending on how fast you could shoot and plot. Then you cogitated about forecast winds ahead, did some of your own guessing on same, included compass errors, a little witchcraft, and made a new heading toward the destination. There was a lot of art to it. Today a sophisticated device tells moment by moment where you are and then what course to fly toward the destination. The fickle winds may change it, but the system knows immediately, makes a correction and tells you about it—provided you haven't programmed or used it improperly or it hasn't had a technical failure.

Still I find the knowledge gained of the stars useful—oh, in a most minor way, but if I'm eastbound at night and the North Star, Polaris, is over my left shoulder, I know I am headed east. Because I learned the stars I can glance into the sky and roughly orientate myself and know, crudely, what the heading is, if the general direction is correct. And if you learned the stars and constellations you were captured by the romance of the heavens—it stays with you, and looking into a clear, crisp night sky, with the stars and wandering planets you know and, at times, have been on very intimate terms with, you feel a certain nostalgia and questioning that briefly untethers you from the earth.

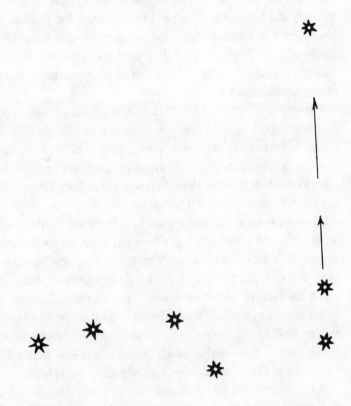

The simplest act of celestial—finding Polaris (the North Star) from Dubhe and Merak, the Big Dipper's pointers.

ADF

Another skill, which seems to be going out of style, is the ADF, automatic direction finder. FAA has been removing radio beacons from the outer marker locations, which is too bad and a big mistake. The omni and DME (Distance Measuring Equipment) system that covers the U.S.A. and much of the world has made the need for an ADF less. But there are radio beacons still around, and broadcast stations. Fly off across the Pacific, or the Near and Far East, Africa—lots of places—and the ADF is a handy gadget. My son and I delivered a Cessna 402 to Sydney, Australia, from Wichita; the ADF was so important that we had two of them installed.

There's more to an ADF than following the needle. You can plot bearings, but to do that you have to know the ADF's limitations, its frustrating swinging when trying to hold on to a distant station, its inaccuracy near dawn and sunset, the need for applying a correction for meridian convergence at long ranges. Learning all that, working with it, gives a knowledge that is useful in all ADF uses; even when making an ILS, with the ADF pointing at an outer marker that still has a beacon, your ability to visualize angles, how far off set you are from on course, how big a heading change you'll need to get on the localizer makes your flying better. Your facility with omni radials or bearings will be quick and better because you have worked with and know the art of radio direction finding. Without this facility the early international airline flying would have had a tough time indeed—so would Louise Sacchi and Max Conrad delivering airplanes worldwide.

ADF approaches are still used—though infrequently compared to ILS and Omni; there are places in the U.S.A. where an ADF is a useful navigation device, a helpful aid. Learning to use it tracking as well as taking fixes is interesting as well as rewarding—it's a skill that adds depth to a pilot's ability.

Magnetic Compass

There would be little navigation—except inertial—without a magnetic compass. While it shows the way and we depend on it, it's a fickle instrument subject to various annoying things: northerly turning error, dip, deviation, to name key ones. So it's obvious a pilot should understand the magnetic compass well and then know how good or bad the compass is in the airplane. The big bugaboo, of course, is its accuracy, what its deviation is—if it's been checked recently and checked well.

TWA determined, when they started using Doppler for over-ocean navigation, that the compass error quality in the fleet had to be improved because Doppler, in the final analysis, is only as good as its heading information. So they set up a major project. To their dismay they found that the compass rose they'd been using was sitting on ground that had lodestone properties! That made all compass checks in error. They quickly fixed that and got the fleet average deviation close to one degree—which is an impressively good number.

How do we use the compass since it isn't dead beat, meaning it doesn't follow a turn degree by degree? It runs ahead, or holds back and then swings past the number when we stop our turn; it is useless during precision flying such as making an instrument approach. To overcome the problem we actually fly a directional gyro heading (DG) that is set to agree with the compass and reset periodically to get the gyro accurate, because gyro precession, with time, makes it wander from the original setting.

Directional Gyro

DGs (directional gyros) are the setup for less expensive airplanes, like mine. More sophisticated airplanes—meaning ones that cost more—have the gyro and compass married into one unit that never needs setting. These are called by various names such as flux gate, gyro compass, et cetera. It's too bad the smaller airplanes don't have this sophistication, because they sometimes need it more than the others; the little airplanes—using "little" interchangeably with "less expensive"—most likely, though not always, are flown by less experienced pilots who need all the help they can get, especially when they start flying instruments.

Why all this? Simply because if the gyro hasn't been set accurately with the magnetic compass heading, there will be a disparity between the two headings and the pilot won't know which one to fly. Setting the gyro is not a simple matter. It has to be done when the airplane is "quiet," meaning level, with no acceleration or deceleration, no turning. It shouldn't be bouncing, either, because the compass, jiggling about in rough air, doesn't generally show the correct heading. When a disparity exists between gyro and compass the pilot is confused as to which is the one to use.

A study was made by FAA of incidents when pilots got lost—most of the pilots were neophytes. Some of the places they finally landed were as much as 150 miles off course! But the interesting part was that most of them complained that the compass or DG was in error and that there were big differences between them. They were confused. I'll wager their instructors never took the time to explain carefully the way a DG is set and the traps therein. Probably a lot of small airplanes rarely, if ever, have the instruments overhauled. A DG in poor condition will precess quickly, so the heading wanders away from the correct heading rather rapidly after it's set.

We should know what our DG's precession rate is. Set the DG carefully and fly for fifteen minutes in smooth air, then check how much the heading has wandered off in that time. Then you know a rate, 3° in fifteen minutes for example. That accomplishes two things: one, it tells if the precession is excessive and it's time to overhaul the instrument; two, how far it's apt to be off over a period of time if you've been unable to set it because of rough air. I check this periodically in my airplane and keep a record of it—if only in my mind.

Heading

Accurate heading is obviously necessary for navigation, and it has to be flown tight—no wandering this way and that, but as steady and as close as possible until there is *good* reason to change it. If the heading is steady we know how we've been tracking—perhaps not where—but the invisible line we've drawn across the earth is straight and consistent. If we say, euphemistically, "our position is hazy," we will know what the errors were when we get a proper fix, and what course to apply the errors to, and we'll go merrily on our way. A precisely flown heading gives a base to work from. Wandering headings, like a person walking in circles lost in the woods, rarely take us over something to recognize and get a fix on. The wandering makes it difficult to orientate configurations on the ground with a map, but if our heading is steady we can begin to fit the jigsaw pattern together easier because we're always in the same angular relation to things. Holding a heading will, like walking downhill, eventually get us to something we're able to recognize.

Time

Big on the list of navigation instruments is a watch or clock. Time is a very important part of navigation. Knowing what our line of position is by the clock will help in getting a position. We know our true airspeed, we know how long we've been flying, we have a rough idea of how much the wind is helping or hindering and apply that to our TAS (true airspeed) to calculate an approximate ground speed. So if we've been flying fifty minutes at a ground speed of 135 knots we're roughly 110 miles from our last position—give or take according to the wind forecast. But that band 110 miles out, perhaps 10 miles wide, even 20, is a band we're in, and on a map that's the area to look for something on the ground we can recognize.

Time has other functions, and none more important than telling, after we've computed ground speed, the ETA, what time we'll arrive at our destination. Why is the ETA important? Not simply to tell passengers how much longer, but for us to know how much fuel we'll have remaining on arrival and a time for weather information at the destination. From these two we can determine what problems may or may not face us—fuel, weather and alternate if needed. We keep track of ETAs and constantly update them.

Plot and Calculate

Obviously if we're going to do all this we need a calculator and the know-how to use it—expertly. Now electronic calculators are everywhere and very good too, but I always want an old-fashioned circular type right near by—electronic ones run out of juice, or break down, but the plastic circular kind is a steady friend indeed. Also there is always a plotter in my navigation gear to plot bearings, measure distances, draw out radials, compute courses and all the rest. Facility with a plotter is a necessary part of the navigation art.

Simple Again

A lot of what we've said here is primary stuff and probably very ho-hum to the pilot who flies a jet with autopilot, flight directors, INS and Lord knows what. But I'm sure that pilot has these basics well established, has known them from way back.

They are necessary to give that solid foundation for flight management—they are a part of the art of flying—there will never be an airplane or time when map and plotter, calculator and ADF will not be useful. I've never flown an airplane yet that at some time or another I haven't established my position the "old-fashioned way"—looking out the window. It's always been a source of comfort, too.

17

Performance

THERE ARE TWO WAYS to set up cruise performance: one, by ball park numbers or two, by carefully checking and setting.

Ball park is setting, for example, 2,300 rpm because that gives us about 130 knots and, give or take, fuel burn of about eleven gallons per hour. It's the way some pilots use airplanes and are happy with the results.

An airplane, however, is more sensitive to its environment: temperature and altitude, strong head winds or giddy tail winds; heavy weight or light. If all these factors are considered and used, whether in a big jet or two-place single engine, you will get more from the airplane, burn less fuel, get there with more reserves and be easier on the airplane. The best way to fly is interesting and en-lightening.

Compute

Computing starts at takeoff when we compute that the runway is long enough, that we can miss obstructions. In airline operation and corporate jets this is done meticulously; in the world of light twins and singles, however, it gets pretty hazy; and probably in no one area is the required performance more ignored than in light twins. They are marginal at best on one engine. Out of many air-ports, their single engine capability—the capability to continue with one out and fly over obstructions—is almost nil. You see them use airports on the basis of what they can get off the ground with and devil take the hindmost if an engine quits. Too bad, but it's their problem, including their conscience in relation to innocent people flying with them.

I'm not going to get too deeply into light twin engine-out performance. Suffice to say it's marginal; that in many cases it's better to chop the other engine and land straight ahead than it is to try and struggle along on the remaining one; that an advertised 250 or 300 feet per minute single engine rate of climb is a dream-world number as soon as the temperature gets above standard, 59° F at sea level—and/or if the airport is above sea level. At best, 300 fpm isn't much. With temperature above standard, field elevation above sea level, turbulent air and a pilot who doesn't have a lot of experience in engine-out flying, the 300 fpm becomes something on the negative side—the airplane will go down instead of up. The number, 300 fpm climb, is computed with gear up, bad engine feathered, flaps up, a 5° bank toward the good engine and cowl flaps closed. If the bad engine is windmilling rather than feathered, on one typical turbocharged twin, the 300 fpm rate of climb turns into a 100 fpm negative rate of climb—that means down! Gear down is another 350 fpm and 15° flaps, 200 fpm. They are accumulative so that if flaps and gear are still down and the bad engine isn't feathered there will not be a 300 fpm rate of climb, but rather a 650 fpm rate of descent!

It Isn't Easy

This puts a big premium on getting the engine feathered and flaps and gear up. To do all that properly and quickly takes practice and a well-tuned pilot. The average day-to-day pilot doesn't get the practice and isn't sharp in doing these calisthenics. Dangerous, however, is the day-to-day pilot who tries to move fast and do all this—while, of course, flying the airplane and keeping speed and control. The chances are very high that the emergency action will be fouled up—which strengthens the idea that if at all reasonable it's best to chop the good engine and get stopped on the ground. (Jets are different, as stated previously.)

This doesn't advocate, by any means, that one should go around cutting engines for practice unless it is with an *experienced* instructor, with ample altitude and under ideal conditions. This is dangerous business and really should be done in a simulator where mistakes can be made harmlessly and, more importantly, the marginal characteristics demonstrated.

But to leave this on a more pleasant note: Engines seldom quit in the critical part of the flight profile and put us in this most difficult situation. But the peril lurks there, and we should be aware of its consequences. It can happen.

It would behoove light twin pilots to sit with the airplane's manual and carefully review what it will and will not do. Takeoff performance from the same manual needs careful scrutiny in relation to departure airports. At least, if the airplane is being flown from a field that gives little hope if an engine should fail, the pilot knows it and can decide if that's a chance worth taking.

Engine Out En Route

The marginal takeoff performance of a light twin isn't the only area to be wary of; think about its single-engine ceiling when on instruments over mountainous terrain. Many light twins' single-engine ceilings are below the minimum instrument altitude in certain parts of the country. Have we planned what to do and which way we'd go to get out of high country should an engine fail? It's nice to think about this in advance and not during a time of panic when it happens.

These are harsh statements and meant to be. A light twin is nice to have, useful and does give some security a single engine airplane cannot. But it's not as great as visualized, and sometimes having two engines just raises the odds of having trouble. Lindbergh figured that out when he flew to Paris and decided that the chances were better with one engine. That's oversimplification because the engine-out performance in those days was really pathetic without feathering props or much excess power available, but the principle isn't far off.

Single

Do we ever, honestly, look at the takeoff capabilities of our single engine airplane in relation to the airports we operate from? Not many of us do. It's worth doing.

Weight Reduction

There's an appreciable improvement in takeoff performance if weight is reduced. It's summer; we're taking a few friends for a sightseeing ride—we certainly don't need fuel tanks.

It's impressive how an innocent airport we know well can suddenly look different on a hot day. I landed and filled the tanks at a small airport in New Hampshire on a warm summer day. Three friends arrived unexpectedly and asked if I'd give them a ride over their house. Glad to oblige, but I quickly ran numbers and said I'd have to make two hops since I couldn't carry them all without exceeding gross weight at the high temperature and with full tanks. So that's the way the hops were made, but even with the reduced gross I found myself noticing details on the tops of trees at the end of the runway that I'd never observed before.

What that says is that just because we're under gross weight everything isn't always going to be peachy; under some conditions—hot day, no wind or a tiny tail wind—we can have unwanted thrills and still be legal.

The point is, again, that judgment comes before just being legal. Remember the rules are made to a *minimum* standard; good judgment sometimes says to do better.

Part of this is found in fine print in those manuals we may study. Little statements say a lot, as, for example, "Maximum performance techniques as specified in Section 4." That's in fine print as a note on the chart for takeoff distance in a manual. I dare say most of us don't use "maximum performance technique" on each takeoff or practice it very much.

Another interesting note on the same chart says, "For operation on a dry, grass runway, increase distance by 15% of the 'ground roll' figure." That's worth thinking about when you're taking off from a small grass airport.

The pros take surface conditions into account. If there's slush on the runway, for example, a weight penalty to make the runway length sufficient has to be taken. Water affects the takeoff distance too. It's no different for smaller airplanes and ought to be in the pilot's thinking process.

Cruise Performance

Enroute, cruise, how does performance fit? It starts with altitude; what altitude are we planning to fly? Each type of airplane has an altitude at which it's most efficient—it changes, of course, with temperature and load, but that's part of the computation.

In jets the most miles per pound of fuel will be at a high altitude, but not so high the airplane is staggering around the sky. The optimum altitude changes as the weight changes, and we climb as the load is reduced by fuel burn-off. We do if ATC will let us.

Temperatures at altitude play a very important part, and one cannot climb if the next higher altitude will have temperatures too high. Performance goes to pot. With jets the tropopause plays a big part in this. Below, in the troposphere, it's cold, but above the tropopause the air is warmer. You study forecasts, decide that, say, 35,000 feet will still be below the tropopause and cool enough to fly at cruise. ATC clears you and climb is started. The "damn it" factor comes in when at 34,000 feet you climb through a little turbulence, the temperature goes from −50°C to −43°C, and the performance isn't there. We've flown through the tropopause that the forecast missed. Cruise power is too slow, you have to keep climb power on, and there you are, as the expression goes, "with the nose at 35,000 feet and the tail draggin' in the water." It's a frantic call to ATC to get back down where it's cool. So pilots playing around in those upper regions take the tropopause height seriously and get as good a forecast as possible on its location.

Weight and altitude affect small airplanes too. My 172 is a lot different and accepts higher altitudes when there's just me and my petite wife aboard. Add another person and my best altitude is about 2,000 feet lower. Airplanes, big or small, have the same things influencing them; paying close attention and planning for them provides better performance.

Of course we pick the aircraft's optimum altitude to cruise, provided weather cooperates. There may be a heinous head wind up there, or a layer of ice and such disagreeable items that will force us to choose another level, but at least we work toward the best level when the factors of nature allow.

Head Winds

Let's talk a little about head winds (the only people who never have them are balloon pilots) and how we'll cruise if we have a wind against us.

There's a popular notion that says, "Use high cruise power in a head wind, lower long range power in a tail wind." That's so you'll get to destination with the maximum amount of fuel, burn the least.

This old idea isn't always true, however. If we want to save fuel, it's best to pull back power even into a head wind unless it's very, very strong. Let's look at it:

Cessna 414A: 20,000 feet, 75-knot head wind:

75% power = 3.9 miles per gallon
60% power = 4.02 miles per gallon

Cessna 172: 6,000 feet, 30-knot head wind:

75% power = 10.73 miles per gallon
59% power = 11.04 miles per gallon

The differences are similar at different altitudes. It takes a little over a ninety-knot head wind before 75 percent power and 60 percent become about the same in the 414, and just under fifty knots for the 172.

In the thirty-knot head wind case, flying a 172, you can go fifty-three miles farther flying to dry tanks at 59 percent power than you can at 75 percent.

Jets, in their realm, have related characteristics.

Perhaps this little exercise demonstrates the fundamental that facts—data in the manual—are better than rules of thumb. We said that navigation is a science of suspicion—that might well be said about all of flying. We constantly need to challenge what we hear, see, smell or think. The science now is a very exact one; performance can be computed precisely for our use. Rules of thumb, while handy for the quick moment until things sort themselves out, do not give the airplane free rein to deliver its full capabilities.

A rule of thumb, at some leisure time, can be checked against what the numbers are so that when it's used we know it's a good rule of thumb. However, we need to realize that it's not the way to go. Computers, hand-held calculators and certain manual formats—some are much better than others—now make using precise data an easy task, and the more we refer to these data, the easier the task becomes.

18

Crew Members

WHILE WE'RE CRUISING let's talk about crew members—first officers, second officers, friends, husbands, wives and children. They can all be useful to some degree.

The crew member we talk about most is the first officer. In certain airplanes a first officer is required, and on some, second officers are, also.

DC-3 Era

In DC-3 days the first officer was an apprentice, there to learn from the captain and not to touch anything unless told to. While relationships were generally friendly, the line of command was sharply drawn.

When the four-engine airplane came into the transport picture after World War II, the first officer's role changed from apprentice to an essential part of the crew. The complexities of the aircraft and the growing air traffic control system elevated the role and demanded more experience.

The second officer originally came into the picture as a flying mechanic to keep tabs on the airplane's problems and then, once on the ground, to help the maintenance people diagnose and fix them.

Gradually the airplanes were designed so the second officer had a specific position with controls for fuel, electrical, pressurization and other systems. He became an important adjunct to the crew.

Change

The second officer position, however, has been done away with in the newest airplanes, a casualty of computers and advanced design that makes systems automatic and simpler. But there are many airplanes still flying that require a second officer, and they will be around for a long time.

G/A Pilot

The general aviation (G/A) pilot, in single and many twin engine aircraft, flies without a first officer. This makes a very cockeyed contradiction to the entire system. Why? Because the G/A pilot, who may have minimum experience, even though he's just been handed an instrument rating and told by the FAA he can fly weather when he's far from being able to, winds up in weather and the entanglement of the ATC system without any help. When I fly weather within a busy ATC system in my 172 I find the task more difficult than flying a 747 under the same conditions! Crazy.

This plays no small part in the fact that the G/A accident record in weather is many times higher than the airline record.

While the G/A pilot may not have a first officer, frequently there is a warm body in the right seat that can reduce the workload to some degree. A little training and proper relationship with this person will be very beneficial.

Automatic Pilot

But before talking about that let's talk about automatic pilots. Simple; every airplane flying instruments ought to have one!

Being on instruments, navigating, responding to ATC, making heading changes, getting weather, taking care of the airplane's systems such as carburetor heat, fuel management and so forth, and flying the airplane is juggling of the highest order. While our juggling capabilities may be such that we can keep three balls going at once, something will certainly throw in the fourth, fifth and sixth balls; then chances are we'll drop them all.

The NASA research data shows a definite relationship between the experienced and inexperienced instrument pilot. Inexperienced pilots, when distracted—and a busy instrument environment is a bundle of distractions—tend to "stare" at instruments and dwell much longer on one or another, reducing overall scan, which degrades the instrument flying. This adds to problems and is one of those extra balls thrown in the juggling act. Attempts are being made to improve instruction and give new instrument pilots better capabilities, but that's not here as yet—it's still experience and practice that counts, and new instrument pilots should realize their limitations because of this lack of experience.

It is appalling to visualize an inexperienced instrument and weather pilot operating in a complex situation without help. While it's hoped that these pilots will use caution and stay out of complex situations, it isn't always easy to do, and what looks like a moderate weather situation can develop into a tough one because that's the way weather is.

With the confused busyness of managing what's going on, little time is available for thinking ahead and planning regular and alternate moves.

The autopilot helps. Our attention doesn't have to be centered on the manual labor of holding a heading, altitude, keeping wings level or turning. Flying becomes a matter of checking, within a scan, that the airplane is where it's supposed to be and the autopilot programmed properly. This is a far cry from hand flying and reduces the operation to a matter of management rather than high concentration on details that leave little or no time for important decisions and planning.

Autopilot or qualified first officer (copilot) should be a requirement for any and all instrument flights. This becomes more important as the level of pilot experience is less. It's almost unbelievable that our system allows exactly the opposite!

Use a Friend

So we're going on a cross-country instrument flight in our Beech Sierra with a nonflying friend along. A little preflight preparation can have this friend holding charts, getting the one you want, keeping notes of times, fuel and so forth, as you direct, and pouring a cup of coffee from the thermos. If time allows, like a session the night before, a lot of explaining and showing will make this nonflyer a useful crew member. If a person flies with us a lot it shouldn't take very long to teach them how to hold a heading and altitude. There's no point in dwelling on it—your imagination can do the job.

There's use to be made of even a first rider by asking the person to look for traffic—especially around the airport—and my pet request is to have the person look to the right as I turn on a left base leg—the possibility of an airplane on a *long* final coming at you from the side is one that always concerns me.

How

How we use crew members is important. The concepts of what they do and the relationship between captain and crew member can create a smooth, useful operation; without them, the atmosphere will be one of hazardous confusion.

First: Procedures are necessary so each person knows what to do, and the other person, what to expect. Procedures are the backbone of airline operation in the sense that I can fly a flight with a first officer I've never seen before, let alone flown with, yet I know exactly what he will do. The key to procedures is to keep them simple, short and needed—superfluous procedures take up time, degrading the attention that should be paid to the important ones.

Second: The crew members must stick to these procedures and not go off on their own without first telling the captain about it. This isn't to massage the captain's ego, but is a safety measure; you have the omnis set up, you fly a radial, but things don't seem to be working out properly; you start looking around and find the first officer has changed the omni to another station to get a cross check, but never told you about it or asked if it was okay. There are all kinds of possibilities.

Third: A crew member must always point out everything that is dangerous. Examples: The captain is climbing to a cleared altitude of 14,000 feet, but forgets to level off at 14,000 and continues toward 15,000—the first officer tells him. The captain gets low on glide slope; the first or second officer tells him—lots of possibilities.

Fourth, and very important: The first officer must not confuse flight management with safety items. How the flight is operated, outside of safety matters, is the captain's responsibility, and the first officer should not "heckle" him with suggestions, especially during busy times.

This has become a problem to some degree as first officers come on the scene that have as much experience or age as the captain. There are times when they try to manage things, and if the captain is a reticent type, it's often questionable as to who is in command—and that's dangerous.

A crew member making suggestions, other than about safety matters, during a busy part of the flight, creates distraction and interrupts serious concentration, because you must listen when a crew member speaks, analyze what was said, and then accept or reject it. If this is other than a safety matter it is a vexation rather than a help.

My request to other crew members has always been, "If you see me doing something dangerous, say it loud and clear, but don't heckle me with other things unless we've got time to discuss them."

Split command is bad on an airline, and just as serious in G/A. It's probably more prevalent in G/A because there are many times when two pilots with similar experience fly together. On top of that they lack any discipline created by airline-style procedures.

When such a setup occurs the first thing to be done is to agree on which one is in command. Other airline rules can be adapted also, especially the point that copilots should bring attention to dangerous things, but restrict suggestions to them. Don't heckle with, "Personally, I'd do it this way." If it isn't dangerous the way it's being done it is that pilot's way—it might even be better than yours.

Use Them

If we have a copilot we should use them. They're of no particular use if we just have them fly the airplane for us while we do all the work—an autopilot does that, and better.

The copilot should do work at your request; "Tune the number two omni to Cambridge."

The copilot tunes and identifies it and says, "Cambridge on number two omni and identified."

The copilot answers ATC radio calls, responds to them as you request; gets weather and writes it down for you, sets engine power, carburetor heat—think of the jobs a copilot can do. The key is, "use the copilot!" If you are a good commander the copilot will be doing most of the work while you think, plot and plan.

It's wise to check the work, no matter how good you think the copilot is; humans are human and make errors. But it's lots less work to do a quick check of what's been done—and it takes less time—than if you had to do it all yourself. With radio, for example, you hear what's going on, but don't have to go to the bother of handling a mike and talking.

Talk

Observing a good crew in action we notice a lack of superfluous conversation when things are busy. Off-the-cuff words or conversation can be distracting, or mistaken for something important. Passengers need to be clued to this, too, especially in smaller G/A aircraft when they are right there with you. I've had a few that blathered on while I was trying to follow vectors and get set on an ILS for approach. It's no time to be tender; tell 'em the simple facts—keep quiet.

Captain Too

The captain has responsibilities in crew relationships too. The first one is to remember that command should not be bigoted; the other crew members deserve consideration and respect. It is wise to let the crew know that you respect their judgment—there are occasions when asking their advice and opinions will not only make them feel a part of things, but may well provide some excellent ideas.

It is important, periodically, to have copilots fly and make the decisions. It builds experience and confidence. But I've never been an exponent of automatically swapping every other flight. There are times of weather and equipment malfunctions that the pilot-in-command should do the flying. This doesn't mean the copilot may not be able to do as well, but during certain critical conditions there should not be a distraction in the operation as the pilot responsible wonders if he should suggest a different way to fly or even take over from the copilot. In such conditions the command has to be direct and unencumbered, and that is best done with the pilot-in-command flying.

These concepts are just as important in G/A, when you have a pilot friend doing the job of copilot. And the first rule is to make clear who's in command—but then not let it show.

19

Weather

WE'RE NOT GOING into a detailed explanation of weather; that's in another book, *Weather Flying*. The idea throughout this book is to try and present basics that will give a panoramic view of the art of flying, from which the reader can choose areas to study, decide where to improve proficiency and, especially, judge when it's prudent to be wary. Weather is one of these areas—there isn't any time we fly that weather isn't a factor.

The first important thing to understand about weather—meteorology—is that it is an inexact science. The state of the art is such that forecasts cannot be expected to be correct 100 percent of the time. This means we cannot fly without having weather, on occasion, turn and do something different.

Because weather is not always predictable pilots must be prepared for unexpected events. There isn't any reason to be angry or thrown off balance when it happens—it's all part of the game, and we have to take it in stride, maintain our composure and coolly go about the business of flying.

Weather-forecast accuracy is a matter of time. We can tell very accurately what the weather will be in five minutes, but five hours from now the chances of the forecast being 100 percent accurate are reduced considerably; five days and prediction is very difficult.

Forecast accuracy is also a matter of how precise you want it;

this isn't very difficult if you want to know whether the ceiling will be 500 feet or 5,000 feet, but if you want to know if it will be 300 feet and not any lower because of legal landing limits, you are asking a lot from the science of meteorology—perhaps more than it can provide.

These limitations make it obvious that pilots should be aware of the current weather and forecast before each flight.

How to get the briefing? Now we run into the complexities of the system. Part of the study of meteorology, in this day and age, is the frustrating art of getting the weather. I mean physically such as by calling on a telephone, looking at TV, visiting a flight service station (FSS) and so on.

The "system" that disseminates weather is such that a pilot should have a better technical weather background than ever before. Why? Reduced to a simple statement, because you never—almost never—talk to a meteorologist. You talk to computers or specialists, such as at a FSS station, who, in turn talk to computers. These specialists have had training in weather, but they are not, except for a rare few, meteorologists; actually their job is to interpret what the computer says and, theoretically, not give their own opinions—although some do, and often do it well. They are likely to be particularly knowledgeable about the terrain and weather effects in their area, so listening to what they have to say in relation to these peculiarities is very worthwhile.

But it's not the same as talking to a meteorologist, and by rule, the FSS specialists are not allowed to modify forecasts, so they are limited in what they can tell you.

Weather, like the rest of flying, is an art of suspicion; we should always be suspicious of the forecast—not in an arcane way, but at least to keep an eye on it as we would an approaching strange dog. What if? and Why? are the key words.

"What if the front moves faster; what will happen?"

"Why is the ceiling going to improve by eleven o'clock?"

If we are face to face with a meteorologist—as we once were in the golden age before computers—when you could talk to them and ask all the What if? and Why? questions, and follow up on the questions that were raised by the answers, you took off better prepared to face weather and its uncertainties than you are today.

Once we had actual weather reports, airport by airport, on teletype sequences that went west to east and south to north, as the fronts do. If you were headed west out of Pittsburgh and there was a cold front somewhere between Indianapolis and Saint Louis, you could look down the sequence, spotting the wind shift, pressure changes and so forth, and pick out right where that front was. The teletype started about Kansas City, Missouri, and ticked off each station along the line all the way to Newark, New Jersey. Running your eyes down the list gave you a picture of the weather. The same for the one that started, as I remember, at Atlanta, Georgia, and came north to Newark. You could find a warm front's position quickly, reading along the sequence.

These were found in weather offices—no FSSs then—clipped to a board, stacked with the past hours also, so you could study them over a period of time and see how fast or slow that front was moving and if its movement agreed with the forecast. You felt an intimacy with weather information and could relate it to what was out there; now it tends to feel distant, separated, as though you really aren't being let in on everything.

Today it's all in the computer; ask for en route and destination weather and you get actual reports, forecasts, winds aloft and lots of NOTAMS (Notice To Airmen System).

Sounds good, and it is, but it's restricted to that route and the reports along it; your understanding seems to be only of that route.

Knowing weather, however, requires broader information: what has it been doing in past hours, what is happening off your route, especially in the direction from which weather comes. But today, ask what the weather was in the past hour, or a few hours back—generally you can't get it. Request reports off your immediate route and you're imposing on an already busy FSS specialist. He may politely oblige or be irritable, which intimidates and makes the new pilot hesitant to ask.

The system cuts down the opportunity to analyze and judge for yourself. This isn't to say we can forecast better than the National Weather Service, but we should know on what premise the forecast was based, so we can watch the situation en route and see if the forecast is working out and if it isn't, why, and what we'd best do about it. This is important!

So where does that leave us? It means we have to take the place of that meteorologist we once could talk to—check the weather from as many sources as possible: FSS, TV, radio, NWS—visualize and examine so we picture the setup, how it's supposed to move and how it is moving.

The weather information is available and can be dug out if you really want it. There's mobs of it from surface to 200-millibar-level charts, prog charts, lifted index, tropopause, winds aloft, radar summmary and more. Our task is to ask for it, look at it, and study meteorology enough so we understand the use and value of the information.

Sadly I realize that only a percentage of pilots are going to be that thorough. The tendency, from impatience or bravado, often is to ask for a limited amount of weather—is it VFR or IFR— and go off into the blue or cloudy sky without much more background than that.

You learn about this sitting through a shift with a FSS specialist, listening in on the conversations of pilots who call for briefings. Example:

"I'm goin' to Portland, just gimme the Portland weather and not all that other b——s——." That's exactly what I heard one pilot say!

This wasn't the only example; there were others, less crude in most cases, but appalling in revealing that many pilots have not grasped the need for knowing weather to the extent they should.

Why Trouble Comes Along

With these attitudes you can see why people get in trouble; if an unexpected deterioration occurs they don't understand why and what to do about it.

Then, when trapped by low ceilings, or loaded with ice, or in the wild turbulence of a thunderstorm, what are they most likely to do? Call the ground for help; expect, somehow, that grabbing the mike and talking will bring a solution to their desperate problem. Sometimes it does, but frequently they are in so deep no one can help them.

Example: Man with 300 hours total, 3 actual instrument, instrument rating, flying a high-performance single into an area of thunderstorms and an approaching front that had airline pilots up tight. He's using his mike asking ATC to steer him through the mess—a job ATC isn't totally prepared to do. Result: a big hole in the ground where he dove in out of control.

Obviously he didn't realize the severity of the weather he was sticking his nose into or the limitations of his ability—or of ATC either.

Another example: Pilot with a new private license packs his family and self in a Cessna 172 and departs at night, in mountainous country, with thunderstorms forecast, for a cross-country of about 150 miles. Result: The family was wiped out.

Inadequacies

Examples like this reveal the inadequacy of our instruction and licensing. We seem to make pilots who know a lot by rote, but are lacking in knowing the realistic things—the knowledge of what goes on up in a troubled sky. The weather instruction needs to be completely overhauled so practical things are taught, such as the importance of how to gather weather information and what to do with it. There isn't enough stress on what the options are and what to do if the weather goes bad. The system of today teaches pedantic stuff and tends to create a "bottom line" kind of thinking that amounts to asking if it's VFR or IFR and what the terminal is going to be for time of arrival—a thinking that takes the forecast for granted and leaves the pilot unprepared to cope with deviations.

The computer tends to make us think in crisp facts; if the computer flipped it up on the screen or tapped it out impersonally on paper, the numbers must be true; if it says the ceiling isn't going below 500 feet it must be so. But that isn't the way it is; the computer doesn't come up any smarter than the science of meteorology.

Percentages

Somehow, in everyday weather forecasting, something should be done to alert pilots that certain forecasts may not be reliable. A way to do this would be for forecasters to show how much confidence they have in a particular forecast by attaching a percentage to it; 70 percent, for example, would mean they feel there's a 70 percent chance the weather will turn out as forecast. They do this in Europe, and it's very helpful. Seeing this you are alerted, if the percentage is low, that this is a difficult condition to forecast and there's a pretty good chance it might not work out. Knowing that, you can be prepared to cope with it; bad surprises don't catch you flat-footed. For some reason, in the U.S.A., there is an unwillingness to admit in public that one forecast may not be as accurate as another. Too bad, because this procedure could help reduce our weather-related accidents.

Limitations

It's also necessary to teach pilots the limitations of their equipment. Just because an airplane has the instruments and radio to fly IFR doesn't mean it ought to be up there under all conditions. First of all we've never faced up to redundancy. Any corporate or airline jet, or seriously flown twin, has backup for electrical systems and instrument power. But most singles don't. Your mouth gets a little dry when you're on instruments in such an airplane, at night, and the alternator goes out. Solid-state radios use little power and may give you enough time to find an airport, but there's no guarantee, and it'll be hectic at best, a real cliff-hanger for a minimum experienced pilot—and that's who's probably flying this kind of airplane.

Ice

There's the matter of ice protection. Fool around on instruments in winter and you'll finally get ice, but most singles aren't certified for flying in ice. I can visualize wry smiles from people who poke off into "some" ice with their uncertified airplane, but it isn't smart; there's good reason why airplanes are required to be certified for ice flying. The requirements to get this approval are tough; a myriad of tests are necessary to determine if the engine can handle wet snow, ice buildup and other things, that the control surfaces can still move with ice in slots and openings, that the windshield can be kept clear—there is a long list. An airplane that hasn't been approved and gone through the grueling procedure may, in some icing conditions, become unmanageable. That's something to think about when flying on instruments, with ice building up and the world kind of lonesome—and your aircraft not approved for ice flying.

The limitations of equipment, what it can and cannot do, what kind of flying should and shouldn't be done with it, aren't passed along to the new pilots and they should be if we're going to face the problem honestly.

More Limitations

The magic of an "instrument rating," and the pride one has in getting it, are worthwhile, and pilots who go through the necessary study, instruction and test should be congratulated and know that they have increased their safety factor and made flying more useful.

But it must be realized that an instrument rating doesn't mean a pilot is ready for everything. A new rating signifies that the pilot has shown the necessary ability to fly by instrument reference, make instrument approaches, fly the necessary navigation aids. It does not say the pilot is equipped to go out in any weather and fly it. There is nothing in the tests that makes the applicants demonstrate they can deal with weather. The only weather testing is a written examination based on the pedantic things taught.

A basic principle is to recognize this lack of weather-flying knowledge and take weather in amounts our experience allows us to be comfortable with. This is difficult, because it's not always possible to pick a benign batch of weather to fly. As we've said, it can turn, and what might have been forecast to be benign may become something nasty. But good sense keeps us out of thunderstorm areas, ice and low ceilings until we've built experience.

Thorough weather briefings, gathering of information and judging will help us stay out of the very tough stuff. If we've briefed properly our chances of flying weather that's beyond our capabilities is reduced—unless we're cocky fools.

Can't Buy It

There is a plethora of wonderful equipment available: automatic pilots, radar, navigation devices and on and on as long as your money holds out. Nice things to have, but a big important point is that equipment should never be expected to take the place of experience and ability. The best-equipped airplane will still get in trouble if the pilot doesn't know weather limitations—and the fancy equipment's limitations. You cannot expect an automatic pilot to make decisions, or radar to weave you through a mass of thunderstorms on its own, or even icing equipment to allow flight through all ice. A certain level of experience is needed to use this equipment properly and realize that it's there to help but not to make judgments. That's why you cannot "buy" your way to experience.

In the Air

The essential point while flying is to keep up with weather, watch it closely for changes. This isn't difficult with the FAAs Flight Watch (officially referred to as Enroute Flight Advisory Service), transcribed broadcasts, other aircraft reporting and, always, the ability to ask for weather. There are many ways, and a study of the Airman's Information Manual, Jeppesen JAID and so on will tell about them. The important point is to keep up with what the weather is doing as we fly.

Give, Too

When we run into weather it's beholden of us to tell about it via Flight Watch or any other handy communication station. After all, what is actually up there is the truth, the real thing. If we all spread the word we help each other.

VFR

VFR equates, in many minds, with simple flying or easy flying. Let us not be lulled into a sense of security over this. VFR is, many times, difficult and dangerous. Staying, or trying to stay, VFR in deteriorating weather ranks right in there with playing with rattlesnakes. The weather accident report that says "continued flight into deteriorating weather" tells the VFR story, tells why this is one of the highest accident causes we have.

VFR flying, when the weather is marginal or getting that way, requires all the craftiness, attention, weather briefing and especially suspicion, that IFR flying does.

The idea that a 180° turn will solve all the problems caused by running into low stuff that ends VFR is false. It helps in some cases, but is a trap in others.

We tend to visualize weather as lowering only ahead of us so that sneaking along VFR there's always an area of retreat behind—but it can and does go down behind our back on occasion. It's a scary surprise when we turn to run and find no place to go! Then we need real instrument ability to climb to a safe altitude, get in touch with ATC and handle all the complexities.

Those who do not have an instrument rating, but know how to do a one-eighty on instruments and perhaps hold a heading, should realize that the use of this ability, poking around VFR in marginal conditions, is desperate and last-ditch. It's far better to turn when things are still VFR and looking good.

So

Weather sums up to knowing it can be unexpectedly different from forecast, that we should brief ourselves well, keep close watch while in flight and realize that flying VFR in questionable weather is a very dicey game.

Weather also gets us back to the fundamental fact that pilots are on their own, to make judgments, to use information, but not to expect the information to do their thinking.

Mountains

IN THE BASIC BAG of flying tricks there has to be an awareness of the terrain we're flying over. Flat land doesn't present big problems, oceans don't either—although in both cases we can come up with a lot of detail stuff regarding weather and peculiarities such as fog and dust storms, heat and cold, thunderstorms and all that. But basically the terrain doesn't complicate flying enough to set it aside as an awesome problem.

But mountains are different, and we need a certain awareness, when mountains slide under our wings, that the game has been infused with additional factors that insist we pay attention to them.

First is the possibility of turbulence, and second, the truth that most mountain country is high and our performance isn't going to be as good as it was at sea level. If it's a hot, above-standard-temperature day, so much the worse.

This shouldn't scare us away from mountains; they are beautiful, and it's rewarding to fly over or near them, or in and out of their enchanting valleys. But they do ask care on our part and submission to the fact that under some conditions, some days, they will prevail, and we should fly with humility.

Mountains demand we be alert to two basic things: one, wind direction and velocity and two, that the downwind side be approached with considerable respect whether we're flying low in a

Cub or high in a jet. There's something for everybody on that downwind side.

When one is low, close to the mountains, the turbulent, tumbling, down-flowing air can be serious enough to make one lose control. Up high, the turbulence associated with a mountain's wave will bounce the biggest airplane enough to injure passengers who aren't well belted in.

The up-wind side is the nice side, with air on the rise that tends to get you up and away from the rocks and trees; albeit that lifting air, if there's enough moisture in it, will be condensed by cooling and make clouds that hide the mountain.

Valleys are pretty places to fly, but if there's a strong wind the turbulence can be devastating, and depending on how close the mountains are, how tight the valley is, the down drafts can be scary, especially with little horsepower to haul one out of trouble.

Mountains close to each other give the wind a playground to bounce against, turn over and, perhaps, be boosted by the adjacent mountain into a mishmash of flows that are not only invisible, but difficult even to visualize. The airplane is battered around, and it's hard to anticipate or guess which way the battering will go. Yes, valleys are pretty, but they can be nasty too.

Waves

Anytime there's a strongish wind—it doesn't have to be a wild gale either—and it is blowing across the mountain, perpendicular to the range—and the wind direction stays about the same all the way up to 30,000-foot territory and velocity increases with altitude—there's apt to be a mountain wave. If there's a little moisture, lenticular clouds will form and tell you a wave is there, but lots of times there isn't that much moisture and there will not be any lenticulars, so a wave can be a surprise if you're not craftily looking for them.

That's an important part of mountain flying—to be crafty about the mountains and the wind and how it may tumble and tumble you with it.

Waves have rotors under them, and down low they can have fierce turbulence. We fly them in gliders a lot, through the rotor to get into the smooth wave and to climb; you learn to respect rotors.

They extend high too, and if combined with a zippy jet stream tucked under the tropopause, they will knock the biggest airliner around with disdain.

This isn't a book on mountain flying; there are good ones

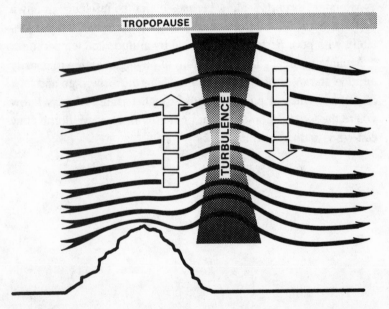

Picture of a wave—at least as it appears after flying a lot of them. Lift on the front side, down flow on the back, under the "hump" of the wave there's turbulence. Very strong near the mountain down low and strong again near the tropopause, where the jet stream is "squeezed" under the trop's inversion. But there's turbulence to some degree in any of the shaded area. This shows one wave; actually there would be another, the secondary, immediately down wind of the first, then another and another decreasing in strength the farther from the primary. On rare occasions the secondary may be stronger than the primary. Waves often extend for many miles downstream of the mountain.

around about it; but since we're dealing with basics, mountains must be noted. What do we do about them? Stay away from that downwind side; watch for waves and keep out of their rotor; realize that altitude, especially when it's warm, will degrade performance so it isn't easy to clear mountains and there's little reserve when prowling around them—think of that when struggling to maintain a minimum safe altitude on instruments!

Jet pilots up at their lofty altitudes have to be alert to wave possibilities and especially wary if the winds are of jet-stream force with a low tropopause. That's a bingo combination.

Mountain airports—high, perhaps under the influence of down drafts and turbulence from nearby ridges—are a bad setup, especially with poor performance caused by altitude and temperature.

Mountains are a game of caution, of paying attention to density altitude and most of all visualizing where the air will go and how it will act when it bangs into the rough terrain. Always know where the wind is coming from, and how fast—if we don't, how can we visualize anything?

21

Airspace

IT'S A BIG BLUE SKY, but if we could see the lines that mark areas denoting where we can fly, or cannot, and under what circumstances, it might look more like a computer graphics display.

Airspace isn't a stick and rudder matter, obviously, but it's a fact of flying life and basic to it. So like it or not, even flying an ultralight—microlight in European nomenclature—we have to know something about it and be aware of airspace and its restrictions.

The less we seem to know about it, the more it becomes an ogre: fierce, unforgiving and ready to swallow up flying freedom in great gulps. We're also apt to visualize the people who set up airspace and promulgate its rules as a bunch whose joy and objective in life is to put all airspace under stern control and restrict any other kind of flying to a tiny area over west Texas near the Mexican border.

Not so.

For a number of years I've been a member of a panel at the International Civil Aviation Organization (ICAO) working on VFR regulations and airspace. Twelve nations are represented from all continents.

The members of the panel are chosen by their governments or organizations—FAA for the U.S.A. Although picked by governments or organizations such as FAI (Fédération Aéronautique Internationale), these experts do not represent their sponsors, but rather are there as experts to use their skills objectively in order to improve and rework airspace and its uses.

When the panel first gathered and I met the people I'd be working with, my old cynicism jumped right in and nudged me. Nice folks, all of them, but mostly air traffic people. Although the majority were pilots as well, I anticipated strong pressures toward more control, with the VFR pilot and sport aviation getting the short end.

How wrong I was. The thoughtfulness and genuine concern for keeping VFR and protecting sport aviation's interest caused hours of effort and discussion. This diligence has resulted in airspace divisions that will leave ample room for free flying, but protect all those flying IFR and operating in certain congested areas. The sincerity and objectivity of the panel members has given me a renewed faith in what goes on behind the scenes—and a respect and fondness for them that, in itself, has been well worth the time consumed.

The key point is that there are areas that simply must be protected by control (to use an unfortunate word): heavy traffic terminals, certain routes and altitudes. Also there are borderline regions where the necessity for control and desire for VFR overlap, and provision for this condition has been made—VFR under control, for example. But even with these certain restrictions there still is plenty of airspace where flying can move about unhampered either to get from A to B expeditiously, or to play in.

What are we saying? The ogre really isn't there. It's only there from ignorance. If we take a good look at the airspace structure and learn the rules we'll find there's lots of room for free flight.

We'll also learn when we must be in communication with ATC and go by the rules. A benefit of this is that we will find a sense of protection, flying IFR, that's pleasant and calming.

Most controlled airspace is in areas where VFR people don't want to tread anyway—by Cub to JFK. When it's necessary to be in these areas there are provisions for VFR by special altitude levels or procedures requiring radio contact.

We can feel confident that most restrictions have been carefully considered and not capriciously created. If we don't feel this is true, in some particular case, we can have our complaints and arguments heard by officials. (When doing this we'd best have a good organization with us like AOPA, EAA, SSA and others.)

Considering the traffic and demands on the sky above, we have a pretty good setup, and the way to keep it that way, or improve it, is by knowing what can or cannot be done in the airspace and flying accordingly. If we do this and don't infringe on the rules, we'll keep airspace for free flight—if we cheat, however, we will find stronger restrictions imposed and airspace lost.

The instrument pilot actually has it easiest. He's under control and knows what to do, which is simply to follow the clearances and information the ATC system puts out.

But the instrument pilot needs skill in knowing the rules and airspaces well if for no other reason than to be aware when VFR traffic is mixed in with IFR and it's necessary to be extra alert.

The system gives a flexibility in that we can fly VFR and then, if the weather deteriorates, call up ATC and request to go IFR under control. This sounds a little better than it is. The problem comes up when VFR goes to the dogs and it's necessary to change to IFR. We call ATC via radio and find no one answers because we're out in the boonies, low in mountains perhaps, and no one can hear us.

In weather accidents caused by pushing into bad weather that has ceased to be visual, we frequently find the pilot was instrument rated and capable of going on instruments, but didn't. Was the difficulty of contacting an ATC facility a serious contributing factor to the accident? My hunch is that it has been in some cases.

Being stuck in a western Pennsylvania valley that was closed on all sides by clouds blanketing the hills and not being able to get anyone to answer my radio calls proved to me that this is a real problem.

The answer? If the weather is that marginal, go IFR from the start. Sometimes we hate to do this, particularly when ATC will route us in a maddening, circuitous way. But we cannot always have it all and must compromise—but compromising in the interest of safety isn't a bad deal.

It all comes back to knowing the airspace structure, knowing the rules and knowing, as well as possible, the weather—then wrapping it up with good judgment. The basics are simple; if you can see and are not in an area that requires some form of control there's no problem except staying in acceptable visibility. If you cannot do this, then it's knowing the system and how to get in it and fly IFR—or landing and forgetting flying for that day.

Descent to Approach Gate

A GOOD LANDING, or instrument approach, begins up there in cruise flight, before descent. The last part of level flight is the time to tidy things up—get things in order so we're free of heckling chores when near the airport.

Cruise is a time of minimum activity, so while we're still in that mode it's wise to set up everything possible; we've said it before and will again: checklist items completed that can be; charts out, studied and ready if it's an instrument approach; ATIS listened to so we'll know which runway and what approach procedure to use. If we're VFR, going to an uncontrolled airport, check the field elevation, the surface wind, which way we'll probably land, any restrictions such as a right-hand pattern rather than left; any peculiar terrain such as close-by mountains, how long the runway is—simple important things, but to be known before descent is started.

Descent is not the time for thumbing through manuals and looking inside; it's a time for looking out! We'll be going through layers of traffic, and as in climbing, it's a time to be careful. We'll also have more work to do: keep the rate of descent steady; change headings, power settings, speeds; tune radios; respond to ATC—many judgments and responses as well as flying.

Descent should be started so we'll arrive in the "working area"—meaning somewhere near the airport—at the altitude and speed where flaps or landing gear can be extended or, simply, the airplane set up to go down the final slot to the runway at normal approach speed.

If the descent is started late we'll wind up near the airport with too much altitude and, because of our zeal to get down when we discover we're too high, the speed will have built up and we'll be zinging through the sky.

It's distracting and worrisome to be uptight about getting rid of excess speed while trying to lose altitude at the same time. One breeds the other; if we're too high it's against laws of physics to descend at a fast rate and not have airspeed increase, yet we want to keep the speed slow—to work with the airplane for landing.

Being in this high-speed–high-altitude bind causes a frenzied situation of pulling power off and keeping the nose up to slow the speed. The airplane just wants to keep on going, and you squirm in your seat wishing the airplane had speed brakes like a glider. At the same time you want to get down—but lower the nose and up goes the speed—a real dilemma. The slicker the airplane the worse it is, and pilots making a transition from a high drag, fixed-landing-gear single to a Bonanza, for example, will find being at the right altitude with speed down to gentle numbers for approach a necessity—and how to do it a new technique to learn. This was a big item when we crossed over from propeller airplanes to pure jets.

ETA–Descent Rate–When

Our navigation has us aware of the time we'll arrive. If we're thinking ahead, preplanning the landing, we know what altitude is desirable near the airport, so we know how much altitude to lose; altitude to be lost divided by the chosen rate of descent tells how long it's going to take to get down; that applied to the clock time says when to start down. This is an important piece of planning, because if we're at a useful altitude near the airport, slowed to a workable speed, the approach or landing is a relaxed operation and probably will turn out well. Basic principle.

The desired rate of descent depends on a lot of factors. We're on top, but going to descend through an icing layer and want to wait until the last minute before starting down, so we'll use a high descent rate; your passenger has a cold so you want to descend slowly; head wind, tail wind make a difference; so does terrain— we don't want to plan descent all the way to an airport that's surrounded by mountains; they have to be cleared first. So descent, when and how, is a pilot's studied decision.

Not Too Fast

Making a descent at high speed, right up against the yellow or making the bell tingle now and then in a jet, isn't the way to come down with maximum efficiency. Theoretically, if you want to save fuel and money, descending in a cruise condition will do it best. Actually, it's a complicated thing to determine exactly because a lot of factors affect the result; what do you want to save— fuel, money or time? If there's a big tail wind up high and little down low you may want to stay up there longer—certainly you don't want to get down too early and then drag along at low altitude and low speed, wasting time and fuel—especially in a jet. These things are what decisions are made of—the pilot's job. But the ball park best is for the cruise-type descent.

This planning is particularly easy to accomplish flying VFR. But if we're on an instrument flight plan, ATC directing us, it seems we're at their mercy as to when we can start down and that they'll make the decision—but that isn't the case if we're a little assertive.

I was involved in the development of a performance-management computer. It would tell the pilot many things to help fly the airplane more efficiently: speeds to climb, cruise and descend; power settings; and when to start descent. Pilots looking at the computer yowled that it wouldn't work in the system. The complaint was that ATC would never let you do what you wanted.

We looked into this, visited air traffic control centers, talked to controllers, flew on many flights with the computer, studied the situation. Answer: A pilot IFR can get the descent time he wants a big portion of the time if he just asks for it.

"I'd let 'em down starting there," said a controller in the Chicago center, pointing to a spot on his radar's scope, "if they'd just ask, but they seldom do."

That seems to be the case; many pilots don't ask because they think it's a hopeless request. So controllers start flights down when they think it's time.

Of course there are times when the controller has to juggle descents to fit the various traffic conflicts or flow-control patterns, but the point is that we should ask—compute when it's the best time to start down and then request clearance to descend. Sometimes it will be denied, but lots of times it will be given. It comes back to flying our flight the way we think it should be flown and then doing everything possible to fly it that way.

This attitude—not asking—encourages the trend for pilots to have the ground fly their airplane. In normal flight, ATC's operation shouldn't cross over to the area of flight management; that isn't their business; nor in emergencies should we expect the ground to take over the trouble. But often the ground slyly works its way into the responsibilities of flight; command breaks down, and two people are flying the airplane instead of one—and the second person, on the ground, cannot do it. The focus of all the problem is in the airplane with conditions and information the ground just doesn't have, or cannot understand. Two commanding will result in a fiasco. There can only be one commander, and it has to be the pilot. I don't point fingers at ATC people for this;

it happens without them realizing it. And, in a certain sense, the offender is the pilot, because he relaxes command and lets the ground do it for him. The ground picks up the task naturally, even though subconsciously.

Take the case where ATC has shut down an airway because of thunderstorms. The fact the weather is too bad along that route was decided on the ground and a while back. When you get in the air, however, you see that the airway you originally wanted, the one shut off, is best—actually has fewer thunderstorms—than the one ATC insists you fly. It's your job to tell them you want the original route even though you may have to argue strongly to get it. We've experienced a few of these.

There are other cases, usually generated by the pressure on ATC to expedite traffic flow. This action occasionally teeters along the narrow border between moving traffic and safety. It's our job to say no when we think the operation is leaning too much toward the unsafe side. Examples are: using runways because they are preferential when the wind or other conditions make it obvious a different runway would be safer; taking over heading changes when you have been cleared for approach because they think they can get you on course faster—actually this can be distracting and interrupt your plan of maneuver. While we cannot ask what each heading change is about, we shouldn't be bashful when their request is perplexing. Another case is telling you to keep a high rate of speed to the outer marker. This makes getting on glide path and stabilized difficult—and can result in a missed approach. If we feel it's excessive we should speak up and say we don't want to do it.

Pilots must assert themselves, must let everyone know by calm but firm action who the final authority is. That's the safest way. And remember, if an accident occurs, or a violation, the pilot will be the one on the spot—all that ground help will have disappeared into the shadows.

This is repetitious I realize, but it's a theme that needs repeating, that needs to be dwelled on. By being in command, by taking the responsibility, we fly better and fly safer.

Approach

Now we're down to an approach altitude and either we're IFR and being directed by ATC onto the final approach path—generally the ILS—or we're VFR and uncontrolled finding the runway on our own. Either situation has similarities. The idea is to get stabilized well enough in advance so everything is checked and the airspeed steady at the "gate" where we start down the slot of final approach.

This is basic and the preface to good landings. Too slow or too fast and the maneuvering required to be on speed at the runway's threshold not only adds to the flying chore, but in some cases makes it impossible—or at best, difficult—because of the dynamics. If we aren't on speed we badly undershoot or land fast and long with all its possible problems.

The pleasing boost to our ego that comes from a smooth landing is really possible because proper approach path and speed control made the flare and touchdown easy.

Airlines have drilled into their pilots the idea of a stabilized approach, which to them means, on an ILS, from the outer marker to the runway, or some point a few miles out.

Stabilized, in this case, not only means speed, but also that the airplane is set for landing: no more flaps to put down, the landing gear is down, the final checklist read—the only thing remaining to do is pull back the throttles when ready to touch.

The approach path, or slot, is there whether visible on the HSI flying an instrument approach or by VASI (visual approach slope indicator) flying VFR, or one's eyeball when no aids are available. It can be a 3° glide slope, or one much steeper, such as on a power-off approach with a small airplane.

Regardless of what slot we want to fly down to the runway, it's obvious that our speed has to be one that has us crossing the end of the runway so a gentle flare and touchdown can be made; too fast and we're fighting to stay on the approach and not pick up more speed and arrive at the runway's end going too fast—or too slow so we're pouring on power and pulling up to regain speed and the altitude we probably lost when, because of being slow, we slipped below the slot. Crossing the threshold of the runway nose up and power on is an awkward position from which to make a good landing.

So we're back to descent and preplanning—do it correctly and it will be easy to start down the slot on proper speed and avoid all the problems of high and hot, or low and slow.

Room for Speed

We don't want to reach our airport area working altitude right on top of the airport. Rather we should be enough distance away to give ourselves time to slow down. The distance depends on how slick the airplane is, and by a little experimentation you can find what it takes, in miles, to slow your airplane to a workable speed. This is the point we really plan our descent to—not the middle of the airport.

Basic Again

We've often repeated, and probably will more, that planning—looking and thinking ahead—is one of the important foundations of flying. This particular part, descent, is a key part of planning—it's the way we set up for final approach and landing, be it visual or on instruments.

23

Final Approach

LET'S TALK about final approach from two aspects, IFR and VFR: an instrument approach, down an ILS 3° glide slope, representing IFR; a general-aviation-type airplane landing at an uncontrolled airport as VFR. Of course all aircraft can land VFR at any airport.

VFR

VFR final approach should be from a reasonable position, where there's enough time to be stabilized on speed and at an altitude from which we can reach the point we've aimed for on the runway with only small adjustments of power and elevator. (Every landing should be disciplined to aim at and try for an exact touchdown spot—good practice.)

The final approach path can differ, depending on whether we're landing power-on with a low-approach angle, or power-off from a higher altitude and steeper approach. (In cold weather, power-off is difficult to do because the engine will cool too quickly—also bad if we're using 100LL fuel in an eighty-octane engine because long periods of idle power aggravate lead-deposit development on spark plugs, et cetera.)

If the approach isn't stabilized and we're too high or too low, too fast or too slow, or combinations of them, there will be wild maneuvering to get to the runway and land. Crazy banks and didos trying to line up with severe chopping of power, or pouring it on in the last stages of approach, will almost assure a bad landing.

If the approach isn't stabilized enough in advance to make the last mile or so—or the turn in from base leg—a smooth, easily controlled period, and if a person is pigheaded enough to keep trying, there's an excellent chance the airplane may be damaged in an overshoot or sideways landing across the runway. If the approach is that badly mangled from the start the proper thing to do is abandon it early in the game and try again.

This isn't to encourage long, low, dragged approaches in single-engine airplanes—a happy medium between high and low is best unless we want to do something else on purpose.

IFR

ILS down the 3° slope: Airlines are adamant about being well stabilized from the outer marker in to the runway, with speed right on and the airplane all set so there's nothing to do except cut the power and land when you're over the runway.

The idea of the stabilized approach is to reduce the workload of the pilot during a part of flying that requires high concentration, and make it less likely the aircraft will get in a condition off speed and altitude that is difficult or impossible to recover from and land. It makes the flying easier. It's really simple to fly an ILS when stabilized. Only small corrections are required, and good scanning makes it almost a ho-hum task. But try getting to the proper speed when way too fast or slow, try to get on and stay on the glide slope, and keep centered on the localizer too—that's tough.

Computers Too

Trying to get on the right speed when not already on it even confuses computers. In the early stages of 747 flying, with automatic landing equipment that included auto throttles, the computers and system did a much better job if you engaged the auto throttles after you had the airplane stabilized. If you engaged them off speed the computer had the devil's own time getting on speed with big throttle changes back and forth—to the annoyance of the passengers—and sometimes never got it done. We quickly learned to have the airplane in the slot, at the right speed, before we engaged the auto throttles—then it would hold speed beautifully with almost imperceptible throttle movement. Newer aircraft and modified 747s are much improved, but maintaining speed with auto throttles has been one of the toughest engineering problems in the development of auto flight.

I respect the computers and am quite sure they can fly better than I can—so if they had trouble getting on speed—well.

Gusty Winds and Shear

We know that on gusty, windy days we carry extra speed and mentioned this in the chapter on shear. The speed we fly down the slot should contain this added factor for gusts.

The point about shear and a stabilized approach is that if we're steady on speed, we'll see the development of extraordinary air or vertical speed changes that indicate shear and be quick to cope with them. If we're off speed, scrambling to get back to it, the changes caused by shear may be hidden in the irregular flying we're doing. So our discovery and response to shear effects may be much later and slower than if we're stabilized. And being slow to respond in strong shear could be calamitous.

Landing

The landing touchdown, after a good approach, is really anticlimactic. If the approach has been cool, calm and collected with speed and altitude on target, leveling off and putting it on can hardly go wrong, and that's one reason we've been so insistent on the area of descent and approach. Of course on gusty, cross-wind days some neat stick-and-rudder work will be needed near the ground, but it's still easier if we have approached well.

Breaking Out

This isn't a book about the details of instrument flying, but as part of the basics there are a couple of important points, and we might as well talk about them now.

The major danger of an instrument approach—and the record will confirm this—is not while we're on instruments, but rather when we begin to see the ground. When we leave instruments and use our eyes to guide us in an environment of reduced visibility, with no horizon and when lacking contrast, we ask for trouble, and we have an excellent chance to find it!

This has been talked of in detail in other books, but I cannot refrain from speaking of it again. It's a real danger. When we attempt to orientate looking out into foul conditions, our scan back to instruments is minimal so we're apt to miss the fact we are descending or banking. It's a terrible shock to look back in at the altimeter and find we've slipped off 100 or 200 feet when we were only at 500 feet to start with!

Because there's no horizon and visibility is limited, a developing bank can easily go unnoticed. These banks we're unaware of change the geometry of how we see and can result in the illusion that we're higher than we really are.

These sensory illusions are part of the "duck under" maneuver that has gained such fame. Yes, some pilots duck down the moment the ground comes into view, thinking they'll see farther ahead when lower, which is a false premise much of the time. But the sensory illusion causes what appears to be a duck-under maneuver, when actually the pilot never realized altitude was slipping away.

Dangerous Territory

Yes, the contact portion of an instrument approach is where danger surrounds us. The answer? Forget the ground; stay with instruments until the runway is *well* in view and you can see a clear slot to touchdown. There's no reason to do otherwise. The approach procedure, precision or nonprecision, is designed and laid out to lead to the runway, and trying to find it on our own, without lateral and vertical instrument guidance, is folly of the worst kind. It is really that basic and simple; stay with instruments until landing is assured and the runway well in view.

The most comfortable instrument approach to me is making a blind landing with automatic control—all the way to touchdown and roll out. It's comforting because I know that I will not have to use my eyes and senses to make judgments that eyes and senses are poor at doing. Coming down the slot you first see lights on the runway, right where you want to be. No requirement to poke around in the gray world of half vision looking for something; no, the thing you first see is where you want to be. The record proves this to be the safest kind of approach; accidents just don't happen on auto approaches all the way to the ground.

Realize When to Quit

Of course few of us have auto-land capability, and we'll find ourselves making the approach by hand or steering via auto pilot, and now and then poor approaches occur. Poor approaches mean being too high or low, or off the localizer, and off speed. The important point about these approaches is that there are times that we can never get back on course from our off set position. To make large corrections as we approach the runway threshold, with big banks, or big power changes, is dangerous and often hopeless. The accident records are replete with scraped wing tips, runway

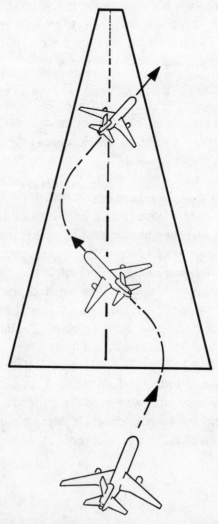

The corkscrew futility of trying to get lined up when "you just can't get there from here."

lights knocked out, undershoots that touch down short of the runway, overshoots that go off the far end, and other undesired items that were the result of a pilot thinking it was still possible to get on the ground and stop. It's wise to realize that no matter how deft we think we are at twisting and turning to get lined up, the dynamics and geometry from certain positions make it physically impossible to get there. (This goes for VFR also.)

Horses!

I like to go back to the old cowboy artist-writer, Will James, who said, "There ain't a horse that ain't been rode and there ain't a man that ain't been throwed."

Well, "there ain't a pilot who ain't made a poor approach or landing," to borrow from James.

The difference in pilots is that the good ones know when an approach is bad and they abandon it. By recognizing and going around, a poor approach is turned into an annoyance; continuing and trying to salvage a landing may result in an accident.

Jack Zimmerman, who came from single engine airmail days and was my first chief pilot, often said, "I don't care how lousy the approach or landing is—it's the recovery I'm interested in."

Recovery can be going around and doing a missed approach to come back and make a good one next time. All this is often confused with ego and pride and shouldn't be. Recognizing we all do poorly some time or other we should shrug off bad approaches—both instrument and visual—and chalk them up as part of the art of flying. As Jack said, it's the recovery that counts.

24

Landing and After

THE OLD SAYING that a landing isn't complete until the airplane stops is quite true.

Stopping is easier if there is a lot of runway ahead to stop on. This means we should get the airplane on the ground close to the beginning of the runway.

It's interesting to realize how this connects with descent and approach, because if we've done these things well, it will be easy to land the airplane on the first part of the pavement—assuming that putting on the brakes and stopping really begins in cruise flight.

Not Too Short

A bit of caution: Landing in the early part of the runway doesn't mean to skin in and land right on the end. That's too close to obstructions and whatever may be in front of the runway, such as a depression with a slope up toward the runway. A situation like that naturally creates a downdraft. Landing short could mean slamming into the up slope and doing severe damage. If there's a strong wind, the downdraft will have a serious effect on the flight path, and we have to be quick with throttle and elevator to avoid

sinking before the runway. This kind of topography is important
to notice and be aware of when looking down at an airport, ap-
praising it before landing, especially one we've never seen before.

Here at Sugarbush, Vermont, the approach to 04 is like that,
and we've had numerous aircraft go through the bushes short of
the runway, some with pretty bad results. Most of these have been
pilots new to the airport. It's obvious that they haven't been very
crafty about looking over the lay of the land before their first
approach.

Glider pilots get pretty foxy about terrain around fields because
they frequently land out—meaning out from an airport, also
called off field landing—in farm fields or what not, and have
learned to look them over carefully from the air before the approach. Any book on soaring will have a section on the procedures for doing this, and power-plane pilots should read and learn
it.

Off Field Has Its Uses

I may be going off on a slight tangent here, but the knowledge
of how to pick fields could be a safety factor for VFR pilots who
poke into bad weather. The feeling that they have to get to an airport may make them do dangerous marginal flying—such as
trying to squirm out of a valley with all the hills around it covered
by clouds. If a glider pilot found himself in this situation, in an
airplane, he'd likely just pick a field, carefully survey it, and if it
was okay, land. Airplane pilots tend to overlook the possibility
that there can be open space suitable for landing other than an airport. It does require knowledge on how to judge a good or bad
field, and we may bend a nose wheel on rough or soft ground, but
that could be better than the alternative of risking collision with a
mountain.

Back on the Runway

Big airplanes have to be careful not to land short simply because the main wheels are way back from the cockpit, and while it may look to the pilot that he has cleared the runway's end, the wheels might not have. In a 747 I liked to see one hundred feet on the radio altimeter as I crossed the runway threshold to assure that the main wheels weren't dragging through the approach lights!

Most ILS systems are set so the glide path intersects the runway 1,000 feet from the end. This is a good distance for big airports and ILS systems, but, naturally, wouldn't be a useful distance on a small airport for G/A aircraft.

The touchdown point can be best judged by the pilot noting terrain and obstructions and gustiness of wind. If the wind is wild and woolly we obviously want a little more margin past the end of the runway.

The basic point is that we want to put the airplane on the ground as close to the beginning of the runway that good sense dictates so we'll have ample room to stop.

A nice surface—and dry day—is pretty routine stuff, but the surface isn't always dry. It can be wet, icy, snow-covered or mixtures of all. Then stopping may be difficult. The question how difficult is another one of those vague areas where exact numbers are not available and it's up to the pilot to use judgment.

Getting the airplane on the ground early is a good start; next we want to get weight on the wheels—retract flaps (get the correct lever), open spoilers if the airplane has them. Ground braking beats air braking unless, of course, there isn't *any* braking and the runway's as slick as it was the day I was just touching down at Orly Field in Paris; 747, on an early, cold, but clear morning. Just as the wheels touched the tower called.

"TWA eight hundred, the braking action is nil!" The runway was a sheet of glaze ice. It took us over 9,000 feet to stop.

In a situation like that, leaving flaps down for a bit will give some aerodynamic braking, but personally I'd rather get the flaps up and try my luck with the potentially better braking of wheels to ground.

If we have reversers they should be used early when they are most effective.

Brakes are best used gently with an off-and-on sequence. Airline airplanes and most corporate jets have antiskid braking. The brakes automatically pulsate off and on for best braking. This way the wheels don't lock and slide. Airplanes don't differ from automobiles in the respect that, if braking action is poor, locking the brakes will not get you stopped but rather will create skidding.

The latest airline aircraft have automatic braking. Once the airplane touches the ground the braking is done automatically, and the pilot just acts as an observer while the brake system does the work—it's the most efficient way and will stop an airplane in less distance than any other method.

Lacking all these nifty modern trinkets—my Cessna 172 doesn't have antiskid or auto braking, believe me—we can be the antiskid device ourselves by using a technique of putting brakes off and on in fairly frequent cycles—every few seconds, for example.

It is a very useful technique, and I learned its value during World War II flying a B-17 in and out of airports along the Aleutian Islands of Alaska, where sheet ice often covered the runways and taxiways. The B-17 was particularly difficult on the ground in crosswinds because of its big fin that wanted to weathercock the airplane—and the Aleutians have lots of wind. But using the off-and-on brake technique we found that it was possible to taxi on ice so slick it was difficult to walk on.

It's a good technique to use on dry runways too, perhaps not with as frequent intervals, but on-and-off gives the brake a chance to cool a little, and it keeps us away from locked-wheel skids that wear out tires. Small airplanes, like mine, have small wheels and will easily slide if braking is done crudely, even on paved runways. Gentle off-and-on helps prevent this.

The real point, however, is to avoid hard braking, and the best way to do that is by landing at reasonable speed, on the first part of the runway. There are many possible difficulties, such as hydroplaning on wet runways, sliding on slick ones, getting off center because of crosswinds and improper reverser use (the airplane skids sideways under some conditions just like a car), but certainly the best way to handle them all is by starting from the most advantageous position—on the runway with as much room ahead as possible to work with, and at a normal touchdown speed. It's basic.

25

Computers and Glass Cockpits

ONE OF THE MAIN THEMES in this book has been the fact pilots must run the show and think for themselves. This doesn't mean we should not pay attention to information or call on the ground for information. The point is that this information should be used as a factor in our judgment along with other factors. The pilot flies the airplane and makes the decisions.

Now, as the computer moves into the cockpit, where does this leave the pilot; how much of his judgment is the computer going to replace?

First let's look at what we have. I've been fortunate in having a chance to study and fly some of this latest technology—mostly in Boeing 757 and 767 aircraft, which have it all.

The term "glass cockpit" doesn't mean we're sitting in a gold-fish-bowl-like cockpit. What it means is that the instruments are glass; the cathode ray tube (CRT) is what we look at on the instrument board rather than the mechanical instruments we've been accustomed to.

What are the implications of that move? First of all, don't visualize the CRT as a TV screen with, at times, its fuzzy picture or poor definition. The CRTs used in aircraft are a new generation, the picture sharp as a knife-edge, with precise and clear color renditions.

Present instruments, such as the flight director, are electromechanical, which means they are mechanical and electrical. So there are chances for failure from either the electrical or the mechanical and from their interrelationship, but the CRTs are all electronic, with no moving parts, and so have a better chance to be reliable.

They weren't put in airplanes just for that reason, but for the fact the CRTs can carry all sorts of information. The information presentation is flexible and can be changed as the flight regime changes. On an approach the ADI, now called an EADI for Electronic Attitude Direction Indicator, can present additional information along with the artificial horizon display. In neat letters, inoffensive and where they don't interfere with your attention but within easy scan, are ground speed, decision height for the approach, a fast-slow speed indication to show where you are in relation to your targeted airspeed, ground speed, localizer deviation, glide slope deviation, radio altitude, and information showing the auto pilot and flight director modes and setup. Before the EADI you hunted over a large instrument panel area for this information, some of it on the glare shield; some you didn't even have, such as the airspeed information showing how far you are from the speed you want and how fast or slow you're closing on it as you make corrections.

The electronic horizontal situation indicator (EHSI) is magical, with separate modes for mapping, planning and VOR/ILS. With these modes there is a plethora of information available, including heading, heading vector, tracks, radials, approach procedures, holding patterns, procedure turns, airports, runway, range to selected altitude, wind speed, ETA, radar weather display, flight path, DME distance, distance to go, a picture of the airway you've selected and your position. The scale can be changed; you can call up all the available airports within a certain area and see your position in relation to them. There's more too, and all in living color.

The colors aren't there just to make it look pretty, although it is like a pleasing modern painting with interesting designs, but they are part of the codes and tell you if the data is actually being used or still in the planning stage. You look at what you've set up and check it before you actually put it in the system for use. When you execute the plan the course line, for example, changes to the color that indicates the data is in use by instruments and auto pilots— magenta in this case. The colors are different also for different functions; a curved line that shows where you'll reach cruising altitude is green. These colors were carefully selected after study with human-factors experts, so the ones used are the easiest to see and recognize, even for people with a slight color deficiency. The lines also are solid or dashed, denoting different functions as a backup to some of the color coding.

Engine instruments are on CRTs and give all sorts of information the old "steam gauges" never could. Colors change as you get toward limits; values are displayed both digitally and in analogue; a moving guide helps you adjust the throttles to the value desired. The same CRT also tells of trouble, warns if a system has malfunctioned and tells how and what it will affect. After the airplane lands the mechanics can go into the memory of the engine-indicating system and obtain the information on failures or irregularities to expedite their repairs. And I'm just brushing lightly over all the things it can do.

What makes these new presentations and systems work is their connection with computers. They give the commands to have the CRTs display what's needed when it's needed.

Computers also make auto flight possible from takeoff to landing and, as we've said, stopping at the end of the runway. They tell the most efficient power setting and airspeeds for all realms of flight and then command the auto pilot to fly them, and the data shows on the EADI and EHSI if you want to turn off the automatic and fly yourself.

Reliability? Its name is redundancy. By mixing failure rates with fancy mathematics, designers learned how many backups were necessary, so the odds for failure get up in the millions-to-one area. You feel very comfortable with the odds, but just to make certain, and my hunch is to calm nervous pilots first facing this new world, there are a few old-fashioned instruments standing by with which you can "get 'er down" if you have to.

It's an exciting advance in the art of flying, and two minutes after you're off the ground you never think about the instrument being a CRT. Learning to use the new systems comes easily and naturally; before long you're giddy with delight about the systems and the things possible to do with them.

Now, where does this put us in relation to the need for the pilot to run the show? Where does pilot authority come in when computers and automatic systems are doing it all?

Pilots are still very much there; it's just that their role has changed from stick and rudder to a systems manager. All these things may do it perfectly, do it automatically, but someone has to set it up and then monitor that it's doing what it's supposed to. The designers, engineers and test pilots that worked on this development never forgot the pilot; with all the glass instruments, colors and information, the EADI, EHSI, airspeed and altimeter are still set up in the old Basic T pattern.

These new systems and presentations give better data than we've ever had. The performance-management system has taken the place of that piece of paper and pencil I had handy and scratched numerous numbers on as I figured fuel remaining, where I could go to an alternate, if I'd have enough fuel to get to Marseilles if Paris didn't open up . . . it was a well-covered piece of paper. Now the computers do all that for you, instantly. But it's only information; the computer doesn't decide if it's wise to stick around Paris for the fog to lift, or go to Marseilles right now; or to Wichita from Kansas City. It doesn't make decisions and judgments that pilots have to make about many things that are a balance of information, a compromise with conditions.

Regardless of the sophistication, the possible feel that all is

being done properly, there are still basics no pilot should overlook. For example, on an instrument approach, the auto pilot is
set up, the airplane is going down the ILS perfectly, but you, the
pilot, still check at the outer marker, as you always have, to see
that the altitude at the outer marker, when on glide slope, is the
same as the published one. This checks glide slope alignment and
whether your altimeter is working properly and set to the correct
station pressure.

This is a basic check, one that should never be overlooked. It
tells the position of the airplane in space, and no matter what the
sophisticated systems are saying and doing inside, you want to
know where you are in relation to outside. (I caught a 300-foot altimeter error on a low approach this way—the ground had sent me
the wrong setting.)

This is one example, but it illustrates the fact that the pilot is
very much there setting up the system and then doing a monitoring job, making certain everything is functioning properly, and
making decisions.

These advances have broadened our knowledge, made flying
more exciting rather than less, more interesting. The manual labor
has been reduced and the demands made more cerebral, a situation which, I believe, automatically creates an atmosphere to
make pilots think better and stay aware of the entire picture of
flight. NASA's work on scanning that we talked about early in the
book showed that a pilot's scan changes with the task; the scan
while flying by hand is slightly different from the scan while
flying automatically. The autopilot-type scan is done with less
time on each instrument because there's no hand-control input
necessary. So it's a very quick glance to see things are in order,
then on to the next thing. It suggests better scan, with time to
cover, check and be aware of the airplane as a system.

Hand fly an approach and your concentration is on one group of
instruments—a high order of concentration; you're almost mes-

merized by the little area of the Basic T. But do it automatically and you see the entire picture; your eyes range comfortably over the cockpit; you check raw data, think about what you'll do if you want to abandon the approach. You're a true commander, not a slave to a few things. Anyone with a modicum of curiosity or adventure will love this new flying world.

Of course there are those who hate to leave the era of flying the airplane. Where's the fun if I can't fly it? Well, you can turn the automatic functions off and fly manually if you want—or, of course, you could go fly a glider, Pitts or old Aeronca Champ.

This is for the big time now, but gradually, surely, it will work its way by degrees into smaller airplanes. It has actually started. I can purchase a Loran C for my 172 that has computer power to tell distances, courses, speed, estimates and position every moment—and all for a reasonable price.

It's the future—pilots will still be needed, and they'll find flying as exciting and interesting as ever.

26

The Summing Up

AT THE VERY BEGINNING we said flying was simple, and then filled the book with data—and we haven't covered it all; that might be interpreted as contradictory to that premise.

But the premise still holds; it's basics that count; the rest are details and nuances—know the basics and there will be a secure place to fall back on.

Take the matter of stalls—are we approaching one, already there or headed that way because of our flight antics? Basics say the wing has to be clean of disturbed air to be safe, and the way to changed disturbed flow to smooth flow is by reducing alpha—get the nose down! That's basic—getting power on and attempting to lose as little altitude as possible are refinements.

First we must know how to fly and the relationship of alpha to stall. Taking off, landing, the entire regime of flight cannot be accomplished if the wing isn't lifting—nothing precedes that.

Scan is a basic, not only to cover instruments in the most expeditious manner, but all the cockpit and the sky outside as well. We even scan with our ears to learn where others are and what they are doing.

Instruments tell us precise numbers necessary to fly by. They also keep us right side up, under control and able to fly weather. Every pilot should know instrument flying and learn the skill as soon as possible in his or her progression of learning to fly. Being instrument-capable increases the safety of flight manyfold.

The airplane itself is part of the basics: knowing how it flies, what performance is and what affects it—heat, cold, altitude, load and all the rest. Knowing the details of the particular aircraft we're flying is necessary to help manage it and its systems—fuel probably being the most important, at least the beginning point.

High on the list of basics is the understanding of weather and what it does to us in the air and on the ground. First the knowledge that it is capricious and always will be and that we have to be prepared for that fact. Then the innumerable effects headed, perhaps, by wind, because its effects are wide-ranging, from slowing our speed to causing desperate shear and mixed-up currents on approach to land. But don't underrate ice, fog, thunderstorms and all the other phenomena—not only what they do to us in the air, but on the runway also.

Navigation is basic, not just to be certain where we are and how to get where we're going, but to know if we will clear terrain, have sufficient fuel for arrival plus any contingencies and, of course, to keep from getting lost!

It is basic to know the system: airspace as it fits your flying needs, the ATC system and the need to communicate with it. Communication is an important part, and discipline in talking— not too much or unnecessarily—is part of the system.

In importance, right next to knowing how to fly the airplane, is planning and being ahead. Planning is part of the suspicion of flight, not suspicion in a mysterious, clandestine way, but rather to make us realize that we should not take for granted weather, fuel remaining, where we are and how we're doing. To be secure against suspicion, we plan for what we will do if things don't work out; we plan and visualize the flight to be, how we want to fly, where and what the reserves and backups are that will assure successful completion.

The most basic part of it all is ourselves and how we visualize our responsibility and actions toward the realm of flight. In its most simple form we are alone. The management and safe completion of each flight is up to the pilot in command.

There is a lot of help available if we ask for it, on the ground and in the air. The predominant point is that help only produces factors—inputs, in the popular lingo—that will help us make the final decision on how things are going to be done. If we approach flying with the idea that others will take us under their wing and safely guide us through to landing we degrade our authority and judgment. This may be subconscious, but it exists and it's dangerous. Count only on yourself.

Throughout this book we've intermixed airline and general aviation operation. This doesn't mean one is superior to the other; all pilots have their strengths and weaknesses; all types of flying operations have their pluses and minuses.

Spending a lifetime in both has made it evident to me that one may obtain useful ideas from the other, and I've tried, in this humble way, to advance that concept.

At any rate, if we've been fortunate enough to be caught up in the art of flying we are very lucky indeed. It's a fascinating world where beauty and science mix and the quest for knowledge never ends.

Index